POWER
FOR
YOUR
LIFE

ANDREW
MURRAY

Whitaker House

POWER FOR YOUR LIFE

ISBN: 0-88368-396-2
Printed in the United States of America
Copyright © 1984 by Whitaker House
Images © 1995 PhotoDisc, Inc.

Whitaker House
580 Pittsburgh Street
Springdale, PA 15144

5 6 7 8 9 10 11 12 13 / 06 05 04 03 02 01 00 99 98 97 96

CONTENTS

Chapter 1

A NEW SPIRIT AND GOD'S SPIRIT

"A new heart also will I give you, and a new spirit will I put within you. . . .And I will put My Spirit within you"—Ezekiel 36:26,27.

God has revealed Himself in two great covenants. In the Old Covenant, we have the promise and preparation; in the New Covenant, we have fulfillment and possession. In both there is a twofold working of God's Spirit.

In the Old Testament, we have the Spirit of God coming upon men and working on them in special times and ways. In the New, we have the Holy Spirit entering men and women, dwelling within them, and working from within them. In the former, we have the Spirit of God as the Almighty and Holy One. In the latter, we have the Spirit of the Father of Jesus Christ.

The Twofold Blessing

We must not think that with the closing of the Old Testament there was no more work of preparation in the New Testament. Just as there were blessed anticipations of the indwelling of God's Spirit in the Old Testament, the twofold working still continues in the New Testament. Because of a lack of knowledge and faith, a believer may even in these days receive little more than the Old Testament measure of the Spirit's working.

The indwelling Spirit has indeed been given to every child of God. Yet, you may experience little beyond the first half of the promise (the new spirit given us in regeneration) and know almost nothing of God's own Spirit. The Spirit's work in convicting of sin, and His leading to repentance and the new life, serve as the preparatory work. The distinctive glory of the gift of the Spirit is His divine personal indwelling in the heart of the believer to reveal the Father and the Son. If Christians understand and remember this, they will be able to claim the full blessing prepared for them in Christ Jesus.

In the words of Ezekiel, we find this twofold blessing of God's Spirit presented very strikingly. "A *new spirit* will I put within you," that is, man's own spirit is to be renewed and quickened by the work of God's Spirit. When this has been done, there is a second blessing, "I will put *My Spirit* within you," to dwell in that new spirit. Where God is to dwell, He must have a habitation. With Adam He had to create a body before He could breathe the spirit of life into him. In Israel the tabernacle and the temple had to be built and completed before God could come down and take possession. So a new heart is given to us, and a new spirit put within us, as the prerequisite of God's own Spirit being given to dwell within us.

David prays in Psalm 51, "Create in me a clean heart, O God; and *renew a right spirit* within me" (verse 10). He then says, "take not *Thy Holy Spirit* from me" (verse 10). Jesus said, "that which is born of *the Spirit* is *spirit*" (John 3:6). This indicates that the divine Spirit begets the new spirit in man. The two are distinguished in Romans 8:16, "(God's Spirit) beareth witness *with our spirit* that we are the children of God." Our spirit is the renewed, born-again spirit. Dwelling in us is God's Holy Spirit, yet He is to be distinguished from our spirit, witnessing in and through it.

This distinction helps us to understand the true relationship between rebirth and the indwelling of the Spirit. The new birth is when the Holy Spirit, by convicting us of sin, leads us to repentance and faith in Christ and imparts a new nature. Through the Holy Spirit, God fulfills the promise, "a new spirit will I put within you." The believer is now a child of God, a temple ready for the Spirit to dwell in.

The second half of the promise is fulfilled as surely as the first when claimed by faith. As long as the believer only looks at rebirth and the renewal of his spirit, he will not come to the life of joy and strength which is meant for him. He must accept God's promise that there is something better than even the new nature.

When he realizes that the Spirit of the Father and the Son can dwell within him, the wonderful prospect of a life of holiness and blessedness is recognized. It becomes his one great desire to fully know this Holy Spirit. The believer wants to know how the Spirit works and how he can experience His indwelling and be brought closer to Christ.

The Promise Fulfilled

The question will be asked, "How are these two parts of the divine promise fulfilled? Are they fulfilled together or one after the other?" The answer is very simple. From God's side, the twofold gift is simultaneous. The Spirit is not divided. In giving the Spirit, God gives Himself and all He is.

It was this way on the day of Pentecost. In one day, three thousand people received a new spirit with repentance and faith. Then, after they were baptized, they received the indwelling Spirit as God's seal of their faith. Through the word of the disciples, the Spirit worked mightily on the multitude, changing their heart and spirit. With the power of this new spirit working in them, they believed and confessed. Then they received the baptism of the Holy Spirit to live in them.

Today there are times when the Spirit of God moves mightily in the Church, and believers receive this distinct sealing and indwelling of the Spirit at the time they are saved. There are circumstances in Scripture which indicate that the two halves of the promise are not so closely linked. This was true with the believers in Samaria converted under Philip's preaching. (See Acts 8:5-

11.) It was also that way with the converts Paul met at Ephesus. (See Acts 19:1-6.) In their case the experience of the apostles themselves was repeated. The apostles were regenerate men before our Lord's death; yet, it was only at Pentecost that the promise of the Spirit was fulfilled in them. The working of the Spirit was divided into two separate manifestations.

What happened to the apostles may still take place in our day. When the spiritual life in a Church is weak, and the glorious truth of the indwelling Spirit is not distinctly proclaimed, the Spirit will be known and experienced only as the Spirit of rebirth. His indwelling presence will remain a mystery. The Spirit of Christ in all His fullness is bestowed as a gift, but He is received and possessed only as far as the faith of the believer reaches.

It is generally admitted in the Church that the Holy Spirit does not have the recognition which becomes Him as being the equal of the Father and the Son. He is the divine Person through whom the Father and the Son can be truly possessed and known. In the Holy Spirit, the Church has her beauty and her blessedness.

During the time of the Reformation, the Church had to be freed from the terrible misunderstanding that man's righteousness is the basis of his acceptance by God. The doctrine that divine grace grants salvation had to be maintained. The Church was to build on that foundation and teach what the riches of grace would do for the believer through the indwelling Spirit of Jesus. Instead, the Church rested contentedly in what she had received, and the teaching of all that the Holy Spirit will be to each believer has yet to take the place it ought to have in our evangelical churches.

There are many Christians who will join in the confession made by an intelligent young believer: "I think I understand the work of the Father and the Son, and rejoice in them, but I hardly see the place the Spirit has." Let us pray that God will grant a mighty working of the Spirit in His Church so that each child of God may prove the fulfill-ment of the double promise: "A new spirit will I put within you. . . .And will I put My Spirit within you" (Ezekiel 36:26,27). Let us pray that we may understand the wonderful blessing of the indwell-ing Spirit and have our innermost being opened to receive the full revelation of the Father's love and the grace of Jesus.

The Spirit Within

"Within you!" "Within you!" This twice-repeated word of our text is one of the keywords of the New Covenant. Jeremiah 31:33 says, "I will put My law *in their inward parts,* and write it in their hearts." Jeremiah 32:40 continues, "I will put My fear *in their hearts,* that they shall not depart from Me."

God created man's heart for His dwelling. Sin entered and defiled it. God's Spirit worked to regain possession for four thousand years. Finally the redemption was accomplished, and the Kingdom of God was established through Christ. Jesus could say, "The kingdom of God is come unto you" (Matthew 12:28) and "the kingdom of God is *within you*" (Luke 17:21).

We must look for the fulfillment of the New Covenant *within*, the covenant—not of laws—but of life. The Spirit of Christ Himself is to be within us as the power of our lives. Within us, in our innermost parts, is the hidden sanctuary where the Law is written by the indwelling Spirit. It is also where the Father and the Son now come to dwell.

In the new spirit given to me, I have a work of God in me. In God's Spirit given, I have God Himself, a Living Person, to dwell with me. This is the difference between having a home built by a rich friend, given me to live in while I remain poor and feeble, and having the rich friend himself come to live with me and fulfill my every need! There must be harmony between a home and its occupant. The more I know this Holy Guest, the more I will bow in lowly fear and reverence, giving my innermost being for Him to adorn as it pleases Him.

The Holy Spirit is the Innermost Self of the Father and the Son. My spirit is in my innermost self. The Holy Spirit renews that innermost self, and then dwells in it and fills it. And so He becomes to me what He was to Jesus, the very life of my personality. Let me bow in holy silence and reverence to say: My Father, I thank You that Your Holy Spirit dwells in me, in my very self.

11

Prayer

Lord, may my one desire be to have my spirit become the worthy dwelling of Your Spirit. Let Your words lift me up in holy trust and expectation to look for and claim all that Your promise means. My Father, I thank You that Your Spirit dwells in me. Let His indwelling be in power, in living fellowship with You and the indwelling of my Lord Jesus. May my daily walk be in the deep reverence of His Holy Presence within me. Amen.

Chapter 2

GOD'S SPIRIT AND YOUR OBEDIENCE

"If ye love me, keep my commandments. And I will pray the Father, and he shall give you another Comforter. . .even the Spirit of truth"—John 14:15,16.
"The Holy Ghost, whom God hath given to them that obey him"—Acts 5:32.

We need the Spirit to make us obedient. We long for the Spirit's power because we are disobedient, and we desire to be otherwise. Why then does the Savior claim obedience as the condition for the Father's giving and our receiving the Spirit?

This difficulty will be resolved if we remember that we have a twofold manifestation of the Spirit of God, corresponding to the Old and New Testament. In the Old Testament, He worked as the Spirit of God preparing the way for the higher revelation of God as the Father of Jesus Christ. In the New Testament, He worked in Christ's disciples as the Spirit of conversion and faith. What they were about to receive was something higher—the Spirit of the glorified Jesus, the power from on high, the experience of His full salvation.

Where there is not much knowledge of the Spirit's work, or where His power in a church or an individual is not evident, believers will not get beyond the experience of His preparatory workings in them. Even though He is in them, they do not know Him in His power as the Spirit of the glorified Lord.

When believers obey Christ's commandments, they will be promoted to the higher experience of the Spirit's indwelling as the representative and revealer of Jesus in His glory. "If ye love Me, keep My commandments. And I will pray the Father, and He shall give you another Comforter."

The Essential Condition

God's own Son could only maintain His relationship with the Father and experience His love and His life by obedience. The expression of God's hidden perfection and being is His will. Only by entirely surrendering to God to possess and use as He pleases are we prepared to enter the divine presence.

Was it not this way with Jesus? After a life in holy humility and obedience for thirty years, He spoke that word of entire consecration, "it becometh us to fulfill all righteousness" (Matthew 3:15). Then He gave Himself to baptism for the sins of His people, and He was baptized with the Spirit. The Spirit came because of His obedience.

After Jesus had learned obedience in suffering, and became obedient to the death of the cross, He again received the Spirit from the Father to pour out on His disciples. "Therefore being by the right hand of God exalted, and having received of the Father the promise of the Holy Ghost, He hath shed forth this, which ye now see and hear" (Acts 2:33). The fullness of the Spirit for His body (the Church) was the reward of obedience. This law of the Spirit's coming holds true for every member of the body: obedience is the essential condition for the Spirit's indwelling. "If ye love Me, keep My commandments," and the Father will send you the Spirit.

Christ Jesus came to prepare the way for the Spirit's coming. Or rather, His outward coming in the flesh was the preparation for His inward coming in the Spirit to fulfill the promise of a divine indwelling. When Christ in His outward coming was accepted, loved, and obeyed, the inward and more intimate revelation was given. Personal attachment to Jesus, the personal acceptance of Him as Lord and Master to love and obey, was the disciples' preparation for the baptism of the Spirit.

As we listen to the voice of conscience and make a faithful effort to keep the commands of Jesus, we prove our love for Him and prepare our hearts for the fullness of the Spirit. If we look to God and are obedient to Him, we may be sure that the full gift will not be withheld.

These words of Jesus suggest the two great reasons why the presence and the power of the Spirit in the Church are not greatly in evidence. We do not understand that as the obedience of love must precede the fullness of the Spirit, the fullness of the Spirit must follow. Those who want the fullness of the Spirit before they obey are in error. Those who think that obedience is a sign that the fullness of the Spirit is already there are also mistaken.

The Key To Blessing

Obedience must precede the baptism of the Spirit. John preached that Jesus was the true Baptizer—baptizing with the Holy Spirit and with fire. Jesus took His disciples as candidates for this baptism into a three year course of training. First of all, He attached them to Himself personally. He taught them to forsake all for Him. He called Himself their Master and Lord and taught them to do what He said. And then, in His farewell words, He spoke of obedience to His commands as the one condition of all further spiritual blessing.

The Church has not given this word *obedience* the prominence Christ gave it. While the freedom of grace and the simplicity of faith have been preached, the absolute necessity of obedience and holiness has not been equally insisted on. It has been thought that only those who had fullness of the Spirit could be obedient. It was not seen that obedience is the lower platform. The baptism of the Spirit is something higher—the Presence that the obedient should inherit. Complete allegiance to every precept of the Word is the passport to that full life in the Spirit.

As the natural consequence of neglecting this

truth, the companion truth was also forgotten: *The obedient can accept the fullness of the Spirit.* The promise of the active indwelling of the Spirit to the obedient is unknown to many Christians. They mourn over their disobedience and pray for the Spirit to help them, instead of rising in the strength of the Spirit already in them to help with obedience. They do not realize that the Holy Spirit is sent especially to the obedient. The Spirit gives them the presence of Jesus as a continuous reality, so that He can do greater works in them.

The meaning of the life of Jesus as our example is not understood by most Christians. He presented the outward humble life of trial and obedience in preparation for the hidden spiritual one of power and glory! It is this inner life with which we are made partakers in the gift of the Spirit of the glorified Jesus. But if we are to personally participate in that gift, we must walk in the way He prescribed for us.

In the crucifixion of the flesh, we yield ourselves to God's will for Him to do in us and for us what He desires. God's will in Christ, accepted and done by us, is the home of the Holy Spirit. The revelation of the Son in His perfect obedience was the condition of the giving of the Spirit. The acceptance of the Son in love and obedience is the path to the indwelling of the Spirit.

Before God came down to dwell with us, it cost Israel time and sacrifice to prepare a house for Him. Believer, desire the revelation of Jesus. Turn inward and see if your heart is prepared as His temple. Seek with your whole heart to know and do the will of the Lord.

Prayer

Blessed Lord Jesus, write the truth in my heart that loving obedience may look for a loving acceptance, sealed by the Spirit. With my whole heart, I do love You and want to keep each one of Your commandments. I surrender myself afresh to You for this. In the depths of my soul there is only one desire, that Your will be done in me as in heaven. I submit myself to every reproof of my conscience. To every moving of Your Spirit I will yield implicit obedience. I give my will and life into Your death that, being raised with You, the life of Your Holy Spirit may be my life. Amen.

Chapter 3

HOW TO WAIT FOR THE SPIRIT

"(He) commanded them that they wait for the promise of the Father, which, saith he, ye have heard of me"—Acts 1:4.

In the lives of the Old Testament saints, waiting was one of the words in which they expressed the posture of their souls toward God. They waited for God and waited upon God. Sometimes we find it in Holy Scripture as the language of an experience. "Truly my soul waiteth upon God" (Psalm 62:1). "I wait for the Lord, my soul doth wait" (Psalm 130:5).

At other times it is a plea in prayer: "Lead me. . .on Thee do I wait all the day" (Psalm 25:5). "Be gracious unto us; we have waited for Thee" (Isaiah 33:2). Frequently, waiting encourages a person to persevere in a work that is difficult: "Wait on the Lord. . .wait, I say, on the Lord" (Psalm 27:14). "Rest in the Lord, and wait patiently for Him" (Psalm 37:7).

And then again there is the testimony to the blessedness of the exercise of waiting: "Blessed are they that wait for Him" (Isaiah 30:18). "They that wait upon the Lord shall renew their strength" (Isaiah 40:31).

Why Must We Wait?

Our Lord uses the word *waiting* in regard to the promise of the Father, the coming of the Holy Spirit. What had been so deeply woven into the very substance of the religious life and language of God's people was now to receive a new and a higher application.

As they waited for the manifestation of God to come to fulfill His promises to His people, so we must wait. Our waiting is to be occupied with the fulfillment of the great promise in which the love of the Father and the grace of the Son are revealed and made one—the gift, the indwelling, the fullness of the Holy Spirit.

We wait on the Father and the Son for ever-increasing inflowings and workings of the Spirit. We wait for the blessed Spirit, His moving, leading, and mighty strengthening, to reveal the Father and the Son within us. We wait for Him to work in us all the holiness and service to which the Father and the Son are calling us.

"(He) commanded them *that they wait* for the promise of the Father." Did Jesus refer exclusively to the outpouring of the Spirit on the day of Pentecost? And now that the Spirit has been given to the Church, does His command still hold? For the believer who has the Holy Spirit within him, waiting for the promise of the Father is not consistent with believing that the Spirit has been received and is dwelling within us.

This opens the way to a lesson of the deepest importance. The Holy Spirit is not given to us as a possession over which we have control and which we can use at our discretion. No. The Holy Spirit is given to us to be our master and to have control of us. We are not to use Him, but He must use us. He is indeed ours. But He is ours as we are dependent on God who gives the Spirit to everyone as He wills. The Father has indeed given us the Spirit. But He is and works as the Spirit of the Father. Our asking that the Father would strengthen us with might by His Spirit must be as definite as if we had to ask for Him for the first time.

When God gives His Spirit, He gives His innermost self. He gives with a divine giving in the power of the eternal life, continuous, uninterrupted, and never-ceasing. When Jesus gave the promise of an ever-springing fountain to those who believe in Him, He did not speak of a single act of faith that was once and for all to make them the independent possessors of the blessing. Rather, He spoke of a life of faith that would always and only possess His gifts in living union with Himself.

And so this precious word *wait*—"(He)commanded them that they wait"—is woven into the very web of the new outpouring of the Spirit. All that the disciples did and felt during those ten days of waiting, and all that they received, becomes to us the pledge of the Spirit. The fullness of the Spirit and our waiting are inseparably and forever linked together.

This is the reason why so many believers know so little of the joy and the power of the Holy Spirit. They did not know they had to wait for it. They never listened carefully to the Master's parting words: "(He) commanded them that they wait for the promise of the Father." They have heard the promise. They have pleaded and longed for its fulfillment. They have been burdened under the need for it. They have tried to believe, tried to lay hold of, and tried to be filled with the Spirit.

But they have never known what it was to wait. They have never said or even heard, "Blessed are all they that wait for Him;" "They that wait on the Lord shall renew their strength" (Isaiah 30:18, 40:31).

What Is Waiting?

But what is this waiting? And how are we to wait? You are to wait for the fuller manifestation of the power of the Spirit within you. On resurrection morning, Jesus breathed on His disciples and said, "Receive ye the Holy Ghost" (John 20:22). They were to wait for the full baptism of fire and of power.

As God's child you have the Holy Spirit. Study the passages in the epistles addressed to believers whose lives were full of failings and sins. "And I, brethren, could not speak unto you as unto spiritual, but as unto carnal, even as unto babes in Christ. I have fed you with milk, and not with meat: for hitherto ye were not able to bear it, neither yet now are ye able. For ye are yet carnal: for whereas there is among you envying, and strife, and divisions, are ye not carnal, and walk as men?" (1 Corinthians 3:1-3).

"Know ye not that ye are the temple of God, and that the Spirit of God dwelleth in you?" (1 Corinthians 3,16).

"For ye are bought with a price: therefore glorify God in your body, and in your spirit, which are God's" (1 Corinthians 6:20).

"This only would I learn of you, Received ye the Spirit by the works of the law, or by the hearing of faith? Are ye so foolish? having begun in the Spirit, are ye now made perfect by the flesh?" (Galatians 3:2,3).

Begin in simple faith in God's Word to cultivate the quiet assurance: The Holy Spirit is dwelling within me.

If you are not faithful in the lesser things, you cannot expect the greater. Acknowledge in faith and thanksgiving that the Holy Spirit is in you. Each time you enter your closet to speak to God, sit quietly to remember and believe that the Spirit is within you. He is the Spirit of prayer who cries, "Father," within you. Appear before God and confess to Him until you become fully conscious that you are a temple of the Holy Spirit.

Now you are in the right posture for taking the second step: asking God very simply and quietly to grant you the *power* of His Holy Spirit. The Spirit is in God and is in you. Ask the Father who is in heaven that His Almighty Spirit may come forth from Him in greater life and power as the indwelling Spirit. Ask this on the ground of the promises. Believe that He hears and that He does it. You do not have to feel anything in your heart at once. All may be dark and cold there. You are to believe, that is, to rest in what God is going to do even though you do not feel it.

Then comes the waiting. Wait on the Lord. Wait for the Spirit. Quiet your soul and give the Holy Spirit time to give the assurance that God will grant Him to work mightily.

As you wait before God in holy silence, confess that you have nothing—no wisdom to pray correctly, no strength to work correctly. Waiting is the expression of need, of emptiness. All through the Christian life these go together—the sense of poverty and weakness and the joy of His riches and strength.

It is in waiting before God that the soul sinks down into its own nothingness and is lifted up into the divine assurance that God has accepted its sacrifice and will fulfill its desires.

After we have waited upon God, we can go forward in our daily walk believing that He will fulfill His promise and His child's expectation. If you give yourself to prayer or the reading of the Word, do it believing that the Holy Spirit within guides your prayer and your thoughts. You have become so accustomed to the worship in the power of the understanding and the carnal mind, that true spiritual worship does not happen immediately. But meditate on: "(He) commanded them that they wait." Keep waiting in daily life and duty. "On Thee do I wait all the day" (Psalm 25:5).

Renew each day your exercise of waiting upon God. The multitude of words and the fervency of feelings in prayer have often been more of a hindrance than a help. God's work in you must become deeper, more spiritual, more directly from God Himself. Wait for the promise in all its fullness. Do not consider the time lost that you give to this expression of ignorance and emptiness, of faith and expectation, of full and real surrender to the dominion of the Spirit.

Pentecost is meant to be the proof of what the exalted Jesus does for His Church from His throne. The promise of the Father is sure. You have it from Jesus. The Spirit Himself is already working in you. Keep the command of your Lord! Wait on God. Wait for the Spirit. "Wait, I say, on the Lord." "Blessed are all they that wait for Him."

Prayer

Blessed Father, we have heard Jesus' command to wait for the promise. We thank You for what has already been fulfilled in us. But our souls long for the full possession, the fullness of the blessing of Christ. Teach us to wait on You. Teach us each day, as we draw near to You, to wait for the Spirit. In the sacrifice of our own wisdom and our will, may we learn to lie humbly before You so that Your Spirit may work with power. Teach us that as our life of self is laid before You day by day, the

25

holy life will rise in power, and our worship will
be in Spirit and in truth. Amen.

Chapter 4

BE FILLED WITH THE SPIRIT

"Be filled with the Spirit; Speaking to yourselves"—Ephesians 5:18,19.

These words are a command. They make us realize what the ordinary, consistent experience of every true believer should be. It is the privilege every child of God may claim from his Father—to be filled with the Spirit. Nothing less will enable him to live the life he has been redeemed for: abiding in Christ, keeping His commandments, and bearing much fruit. Yet, few believers have thought it was possible to keep this command.

This commandment to be filled with the Spirit has often been misunderstood. On the day of Pentecost, being filled with the Spirit was accompanied with the manifest enthusiasm of a supernatural joy and power. Such a state has been looked on as one of excitement and strain, quite inconsistent with the quiet course of ordinary life.

The suddenness of the outward manifestation has been linked with the idea of being filled with the Spirit. Many believers thought it was something for special occasions, a blessing only possible to a very few. Christians felt as if they could not venture to fix their hopes so high. And if the blessing were given to them, they felt it would be impossible in their circumstances to maintain or to manifest it.

However, this commandment is indeed for every believer today. The promise and the power are also for every believer. May our meditation on God's Word awaken in the heart of every reader the firm assurance that this privilege is meant for him.

Two Ways Of Being Filled

South Africa often suffers from drought. There are two kinds of dams or reservoirs made for catching and storing water. On some farms there is a natural spring, but its flow is too small to use for irrigating the fields. So a reservoir is made for collecting the water. The filling of the reservoir is the result of the gentle, quiet inflow from the spring day and night. Some farms have no spring at all.

The reservoir is built in the bed of a stream or in a valley where, when rain falls, the water can be collected. The filling of the reservoir with a heavy fall of rain is often the work of a very few hours. It is accompanied with a rush and violence that can be dangerous. The noiseless supply of the spring is more reliable, because the supply is permanent. In places where rainfall is uncertain, a reservoir may stand empty for months or years.

The fullness of the Spirit comes in the same way.

The Spirit can come as it did on the day of Pentecost, like a revival suddenly filling people with the Holy Spirit. In the enthusiasm and the joy of newly-found salvation, the power of the Spirit is undeniably present.

And yet, for those who receive it in this way, there are special dangers. The blessing is often too dependent on the fellowship with others, or it extends only to the more easily reached currents of the soul's life. The sudden is often the superficial. The depths of the will and the inner life have not been reached.

There are other Christians who have never been partakers of such a powerful experience. Nevertheless, the fullness of the Spirit is distinctly seen in their deep and intense devotion to Jesus. They walk in the light of His countenance and the consciousness of His Holy Presence. They live a blameless life of simple trust and obedience which gives self-sacrificing love to all around.

Which of these is the true way of being filled with the Spirit? The answer is easy. There are farms on which both kinds of reservoirs are found next to each other. There are even reservoirs in which both ways of filling with water are used. The regular, quiet, daily inflowing keeps them supplied in times of great drought. In time of rain, they are ready to receive and store up large supplies.

There are Christians who are not content except with special, mighty visitations of the Spirit. They look for the rushing mighty wind with floods outpoured and the baptism of fire. There are others to whom the fountain springing up from within and quietly streaming forth appears the true type of the Spirit's work. Happy are they who can recognize God in both ways and keep themselves always ready to be blessed in whichever way He comes.

What are now the conditions of this fullness of the Spirit? God's Word has one answer—faith. It is faith alone that sees and receives the invisible, that sees and receives God Himself. The cleansing from sin and the loving surrender to obedience are the fruit of faith. This faith saw what sin was and accepted what the blood, the will, and the love of God could do.

I'm not speaking of these when I refer to being filled with the Spirit. This verse is for believers who have been faithful in their seeking to obey and yet do not have what they long for. By faith they must see what needs to be cast out of their lives.

All filling needs emptying. I *am not* speaking of the cleansing of sin and the surrender to full obedience. That is always the first step of faith. I *am* speaking about believers who think they have done what God demands in this and yet fail to receive the blessing.

Conditions For Filling

The first condition of all filling is emptiness. A reservoir is a hole, a great empty place prepared, waiting, thirsting, crying for the water to come. Any true, abiding fullness of the Spirit is preceded by emptying. One person said, "I sought the blessing long and earnestly, and I wondered why it did not come. At last I realized it was because there was no room in my heart."

In such emptying of ourselves, there are various elements we must have. There must be a deep dissatisfaction with the religion we have had up to now. There must be an awareness of how much our religion has been the wisdom and work of the flesh. We must give up all that has been kept in our own hands and management, in which self has reigned. We must surrender, in poverty of spirit, to wait on the Lord in His great mercy and power.

With a great longing, we must pray without ceasing for the Father to fulfill His promise in us and take full possession of us within. Such an emptying is the way to the filling. With this is needed faith which accepts and receives the gift. It is through faith in Christ and in the Father that the divine fullness will flow into us.

To the Ephesians, Paul gave the command, "Be filled with the Spirit." Paul also said, "In Christ. . .ye believed, ye were sealed with that Holy Spirit of promise" (Ephesians 1:12,13). The command refers to what they had already received: the fountain was within them. It had to be opened up and a way made for it. Then it would spring up and fill their being.

Yet, this was not in their own power. Jesus had said, "He that believeth on Me, out of his belly shall flow rivers of living water" (John 7:38). The fullness of the Spirit is in Jesus, and the receiving of Him must be in the unbroken continuity of a real life-fellowship. The ceaseless inflow of the sap from Him, the living Vine, must be met by the ceaseless receiving by faith of the fountain within us. It is by faith in Jesus that the inflow of the Spirit will grow stronger until it overflows from our life.

Our faith in Jesus will not dispense with faith in the Father's special gift. We must still pray for renewed fulfillment of His promise. The Ephesians had the Spirit within them as their inheritance. However, Paul prays to the Father, "That He would grant you, according to the riches of His glory, to be strengthened with might by His Spirit in the inner man" (Ephesians 3:16).

This verse indicates an act, something done at once. The expression "according to the riches of His glory" indicates something which is to be a special act of divine love and power. The Ephesians had the Spirit indwelling. Paul prayed that the Father might give them a life in the love that passes knowledge. He prayed that being filled with the fullness of God might be their blessed, personal experience.

When the flood came in Noah's time, the windows of heaven and the fountains of the great deep were opened together. This is still true in the fulfillment of the promise of the Spirit: "I will pour. . .floods upon the dry ground" (Isaiah 44:3). We must have a deep, clear faith in the indwelling Spirit and simply wait on Him. Then the Spirit will come down from the heart of the Father directly into the heart of His waiting child.

Faith To Be Filled

There is one more aspect in which this fullness comes to our faith. God loves to appear in lowly and unlikely ways to clothe Himself in the garment of humility which He wants His children to wear. The Kingdom of heaven is like a seed. "The kingdom of heaven is like to a grain of mustard seed, which a man took, and sowed in his field" (Matthew 4:31). Only faith can know the glory there is in its smallness.

It was this way in the dwelling of the Son on earth. It is this way in the indwelling of the Spirit in the heart. The Spirit asks to be believed in, even when nothing is seen or felt. Believe that the fountain that springs up and flows forth in living streams is within you. Believe even when all appears dry.

Take time to retire into the inner chamber of the heart, and then send up praise and offer worship to God with the assurance of the Holy Spirit within. Take time to be still and let the Spirit Himself fill your spirit with this most spiritual and heavenly of all truths—that He dwells within you. His temple, His hidden dwelling place, is in our life, deeper than we can see and feel. It is not in the thoughts or feelings first.

When faith knows that it has what it has asked, it can afford to be patient and be thankful even when the flesh would murmur. Faith can trust the unseen Jesus and the hidden Spirit. Faith believes in that little and unlikely seed, the smallest of all seeds. It can trust and give glory to Him who is able to do exceeding abundantly above all we can think.

Faith can mightily strengthen the inner man just when all appears feeble and ready to faint. Do not expect fullness of the Spirit according to your human reasoning.

The Spirit comes just as the Son of God came— without form or comeliness, in a way that is folly to human wisdom.

Expect divine strength in great weakness. Become a fool to receive the divine wisdom which the Spirit teaches. Be willing to be nothing, because God chooses the things that are weak to bring to nothing the things that are strong. Learn not to glory in the flesh, but to glory in the Lord. With deep joy in a life of daily obedience and childlike simplicity, you will know what it is to be filled with the Spirit.

Being filled with the Spirit is not in the emotions of power or joy. The filling of the Spirit must be sought in the life—in the hidden, innermost part, deeper than knowledge or feeling. The Spirit fills that part of us to which faith gives access, where we *are* and *have* before we know or feel. If you want to know what it is to be filled with the Spirit—see Jesus. Look at Him on the last night washing the disciples' feet.

In the deep calm of the consciousness that He was of God, see the fullness of the Spirit. Seek it in this way. In due time, it will break out in your testimony, in your fellowship with believers, and in your burden for saving the lost. It is only in the fellowship of the Body, its building up in love, that the Spirit reveals His presence.

Jesus said the Spirit will bear witness, and "ye also shall bear witness." (See John 15:26,27.) It is in action on our part, in obedience, that the reality of the Spirit's presence comes. "And they were all filled with the Holy Ghost, and began to speak with other tongues" (Acts 2:4). Having this same Spirit of faith, we must also speak out. The fountain must spring up. The stream must flow. Silence is death.

Do not grieve the Holy Spirit, but be filled with the Holy Spirit. We cannot provide the life or the growth, but we can remove the hindrance. We can yield to obedience. We can turn from the flesh to wait on God. We can yield to the Spirit as far as we know God's will: *the filling comes from above.*

Wait for the filling, tarrying at the footstool of the throne in much prayer. And as you pray, turn inward and believe that the unseen power has indeed taken possession of your whole being. "Be filled with the Spirit."

It is the duty, the calling, the privilege of every believer. It is a divine possibility, in virtue of the command; it is a divine certainty, in the power of faith. Lord, hasten the day when every believer will believe this!

Prayer

Blessed Father, I thank You that the Holy Spirit is to us the bearer of the fullness of Jesus. Make me full. Let the Holy Spirit take and keep possession of my deepest, innermost life. Let Your Spirit fill my spirit. Let the fountain flow through all my soul's affections and powers. Let it flow out through my lips, speaking Your praise and love. Let my body be Your temple full of the divine life.

Lord God, I believe You have given it to me. I accept it as mine. Grant that throughout Your Church, the fullness of the Spirit may be sought and found, may be known and proved. Lord Jesus, our glorified King, let Your Church be full of the Holy Spirit. Amen.

Chapter 5

THE BAPTISM OF THE SPIRIT

"John bare record, saying. . . .he that sent me to baptize with water, the same said unto me, Upon whom thou shalt see the Spirit descending, and remaining on him, the same is he which baptizeth with the Holy Ghost"—John 1:32,33.

There were two things that John the Baptist preached concerning the person of Christ. First, Christ was the "Lamb of God which taketh away the sin of the world" (John 1:29). Second, Christ would baptize His disciples with the Holy Spirit and with fire. The blood of the Lamb and the baptism of the Spirit were the two central truths of his preaching. They are, indeed, inseparable. The Church cannot do her work in power, nor can the Lord be glorified in her, unless the blood as the foundationstone and the Spirit as the cornerstone are fully preached.

The Beginning And End Of Redemption

The preaching of the Lamb of God, of His suffering and of pardon and peace through Him, is often preached in our churches. However, the more inward spiritual truth of the baptism, indwelling, and guidance of the Holy Spirit is often neglected. The pouring out of the blood took place upon earth. It was something visible and not difficult to understand. The pouring out of the Spirit was a divine and hidden mystery. The shedding of the blood was for the ungodly and rebellious.

The gift of the Spirit was given for the loving and obedient disciple. It is no wonder, when the Church is not intense in her devotion to her Lord, that the preaching of the baptism of the Spirit finds less acceptance than redemption and forgiveness.

Yet, God does not want it to be this way. The Old Testament promise had spoken of God's Spirit within us. John the Baptist did not preach the Lamb of God without telling why it was that we were to be redeemed and how God's high purpose was to be fulfilled in us. Sin was not only guilt and condemnation. It was defilement and death. Sin had incurred the loss of God's favor and made us unfit for divine fellowship. And, without this fellowship, the love of God that had created man could not be content. God wanted to have us for Himself—our hearts and affections, our innermost personality, our very self, a home for His love to rest in, a temple for His worship.

The preaching of John included both the beginning and the end of redemption. The blood of the Lamb was to cleanse God's Temple and restore His throne within man's heart. Nothing less than the baptism and indwelling of the Spirit could satisfy the heart of either God or man.

Jesus Himself showed what baptism of the Spirit meant. He would only give what He Himself had received. Because the Spirit lived in Him, He could baptize with the Spirit. What did the Spirit descending and abiding on Him mean? He had been begotten of the Holy Spirit.

In the power of the Spirit, He had grown up a holy child and youth. He had entered manhood free from sin. Now He comes to John to give Himself to fulfill all righteousness by submitting to the baptism of repentance. And now, as the reward of His obedience, as the Father's seal of approval on His having yielded to the control of the Spirit, Jesus receives a new communication of the power of the heavenly life.

Beyond what He had yet experienced, the Father's indwelling presence and power takes possession of Jesus and equips Him for His work. The leading and the power of the Spirit become His more consciously than before. "And Jesus being full of the Holy Ghost returned from Jordan, and was led by the Spirit into the wilderness" (Luke 4:1). "And Jesus returned in the power of the Spirit into Galilee: and there went out a fame of Him through all the region round about" (Luke 4:14). He is now anointed with the Holy Spirit and with power.

Although He is now baptized Himself, He cannot yet baptize others. He must first, in the power of His baptism, meet temptation and overcome it.

He must learn obedience and, through the eternal Spirit, offer Himself as a sacrifice unto God and His will. Then only would He receive afresh the Holy Spirit as the reward of obedience with the power to baptize all who belong to Him.

What Is The Baptism Of The Holy Spirit?

What we see in Jesus teaches us what the baptism of the Spirit is. It is not the grace by which we turn to God, become reborn, and seek to live as God's children. When Jesus reminded His disciples (Acts 1:5) of John's prophecy, they were already partakers of this grace. Their baptism with the Spirit meant something more.

It was to be to them the conscious presence of their glorified Lord come back from heaven to dwell in their hearts. It was to be their participation in the power of His new life. It was to them a baptism of joy and power in their living fellowship with Jesus on the throne of glory.

All that the disciples were further to receive of wisdom, courage, and holiness was rooted in the relationship between the Spirit and Jesus. What the Spirit had been to Jesus when He was baptized, as the living bond with the Father's power and presence, He was to be to them. Through Him, the Son was to manifest Himself, and Father and Son were to make their abode with them.

"Upon whom thou shalt see the Spirit descending, and remaining in Him, the same is He which baptizeth with the Holy Ghost." This word comes to us as well as to John. We want to know what the baptism of the Spirit means; how we are to receive it; from whom we are to receive it. To understand these things we must see *the One* upon whom the Spirit descended and remained.

We must see Jesus baptized with the Holy Spirit. We must try to understand why He needed it; how He was prepared for it; how He yielded to it; and how in its power He died His death and was raised again. What Jesus has to give us, He first received and personally appropriated for Himself. What He received and won for Himself is available for us. He will make it our very own.

In regard to this baptism of the Spirit there are questions that we may not find easy to answer, and to which all will not give the same answer. Was the outpouring of the Spirit at Pentecost the complete fulfillment of the promise? Was that the only baptism of the Spirit, given once and for all to the newborn Church?

The Holy Spirit came upon the disciples in the fourth chapter of Acts, on the Samaritans in chapter eight, on the heathen in the house of Cornelius in chapter ten, and on the twelve disciples at Ephesus in chapter nineteen. These incidents must also be regarded as separate fulfillments of the words, ''He shall baptize you with the Holy Ghost'' (Matthew 3:11).

Is the sealing of the Spirit given to each believer when he is born again to be considered as his baptism of the Spirit? Or is it, as some say, a distinct, definite blessing to be received later on? Is it a blessing given only once, or can it be repeated and renewed?

Our study of God's Word will help us to solve these difficulties. We must not allow ourselves to be overly concerned with these minor points at the beginning. Instead, let us fix our whole hearts on the great spiritual lessons that God would have us learn from the preaching of the baptism of the Holy Spirit.

Why The Baptism?

This baptism of the Holy Spirit is the crown and glory of Jesus' work. We need it, and must know that we have it, if we are to live the true Christian life. Jesus needed it. Christ's loving, obedient disciples needed it. We need it also.

It is something more than the working of the Spirit in rebirth. It is the personal Spirit of Christ making Himself present within us, always living in the heart in the power of His glorified nature, as He is exalted above every enemy. It is the Spirit of the life of Christ Jesus making us free from the law of sin and death and bringing us, as a personal experience, into the freedom from sin to which Christ redeemed us.

However, many who have experienced rebirth do not possess or enjoy this blessing. The baptism of the Spirit is the endowment with power to fill us with boldness and give the victory over the world and every enemy. It is the fulfillment of what God meant in His promise: "I will dwell in them, and walk in them" (2 Corinthians 6:16). Let us ask the Father to reveal to us all that His love

42

meant for us, until our souls are filled with the glory of the thought: He baptizes with the Holy Spirit.

The Living Water Flows

It is Jesus who baptizes with the Holy Spirit. It is only in the fellowship of Jesus, in faithful obedience to Him, that a baptized life can be received or maintained or renewed. "He that believeth on Me," Jesus said, "out of his belly shall flow rivers of living water" (John 7:38).

The one thing we need is living faith in the indwelling Jesus, then the living water will surely and freely flow. Faith is the instinct of the new nature by which it recognizes and receives its divine food and drink.

Let us especially remember one thing: only he that is faithful in the least will be made ruler over much. "And He said unto him, Well, thou good servant: because thou hast been faithful in a very little, have thou authority over ten cities" (Luke 19:17). Be very faithful to what you already have and know of the Spirit's working. With deep reverence, regard yourself as God's holy temple. Wait for and listen to the gentlest whispering of God's Spirit within you. Listen especially to the conscience, which has been cleansed in the blood. Keep that conscience very clean by simple, childlike obedience. There may be much involuntary sin in your heart which makes you feel powerless. Deeply humble yourself and, when the sin occurs, be cleansed in the blood.

43

As far as your voluntary actions are concerned, tell the Lord Jesus every day that you will do all that you know is pleasing to Him. Yield to the warnings of your conscience when you fail. Then come again, have hope in God, and renew the vow: What I know God wants me to do, I will do. Humbly ask and wait for guidance every morning. Soon the Spirit's voice will become better known, and His strength will be felt.

Jesus taught the disciples three years, and then the blessing came. Be His loving, obedient disciple, and believe in Him who is full of the Spirit. Then you will also be prepared for the fullness of the blessing of the baptism of the Spirit.

Let us connect in our faith the double truth that John the Baptist preached: Jesus the Lamb—taking away sin; Jesus the anointed—baptizing with the Spirit. It was only in virtue of His shedding His blood that He received the Spirit to shed forth. It is as the cross is preached that the Spirit works. If I believe and receive the precious blood that cleanses from all sin, I can claim the anointing of the Spirit. The blood and the oil go together. I need both. I have them both in Jesus, the Lamb on the throne.

Prayer

Blessed Lord Jesus, with my whole heart I worship You as the baptizer with the Holy Spirit. Reveal Yourself to me, that I may know what I can expect from You. My Holy Lord, I thank You that the Holy Spirit is also in me. Give me the full, overflowing measure You have promised. Let Him be to me the full, unceasing revelation of Your presence in my heart. Lord Jesus, baptize me and fill me with the Holy Spirit. Amen.

Chapter 6

A DIVINE OUTPOURING

"And when the day of Pentecost was fully come. . . .they were all filled with the Holy Ghost, and began to speak with other tongues as the Spirit gave them utterance"—Acts 2:1,4.

The work of Christ points to the outpouring of the Holy Spirit. The preliminary stages were: the mystery of the incarnation in Bethlehem; the great redemption accomplished on Calvary; the revelation of Christ as the Son of God by the resurrection; and His entrance into glory in the ascension. Their goal and their crown was the coming down of the Holy Spirit.

The Church has hardly acknowledged this and has not seen that the glory of Pentecost is the highest glory of the Father and the Son. That is why the Holy Spirit has not yet been able to reveal and glorify the Son in the Church as He would like. Let us see if we can realize what Pentecost means.

God made man in His own image and for His likeness with the distinct purpose that he should become like Himself. Man was to be a temple for God to dwell in. He was to become the home in which God could rest. The close, intimate union with man was what the Holy One longed for and looked forward to.

What was symbolized in the temple in Israel became a divine reality in Jesus of Nazareth. There was a human nature in Jesus, possessed by the divine Spirit. God would have it so with all men who accept Jesus and His Spirit as their life.

Christ's death was to remove the curse and power of sin and make it possible for man to receive His Spirit. His resurrection was the entrance of a perfected human nature into the life of Deity, the divine Spirit-life. At His ascension, He was admitted as man into the very glory of God—the participation by human nature of perfect fellowship with God in glory in the unity of the Spirit.

And yet, with all this, the work was not yet complete. God's main purpose was still not fulfilled. How could the Father dwell in men even as He had dwelt in Christ? This was the great question to which Pentecost gives the answer.

The New Spirit

The Holy Spirit is sent forth in a new character and a new power, such as He never had before. In creation and nature, He came forth from God as the Spirit of life. In the creation of man, He especially acted as the power in which man's God-likeness was based. After man's fall, the Spirit still testified for God. In Israel, He appeared as the Spirit of the theocracy, distinctly inspiring and equipping certain men for their work. In Jesus Christ, He came as the Spirit of the Father given to Him without measure. All these are manifestations in different degrees of one and the same Spirit.

But now comes the long-promised and entirely new manifestation of the divine Spirit. The Spirit that has dwelt in the obedient life of Jesus Christ has taken up His human spirit into perfect fellowship and unity with Himself. He is now the Spirit of the exalted God-man. The man Christ Jesus enters the glory of God and the full fellowship of that Spirit-life in which God dwells. He receives from the Father the right to send forth His Spirit into His disciples—to descend Himself in the Spirit and dwell in them.

The Spirit comes in a new power which had not been possible before because Jesus had not been crucified or glorified. This new power is the very Spirit of the glorified Jesus. The work of the Son and the longing of the Father received its fulfillment. Man's heart has become the home of his God.

The mystery of the incarnation at Bethlehem is indeed glorious. A pure, holy body was formed for the Son of God. In that body the Holy Spirit dwelt. This is indeed a miracle of divine power. This is a mystery of grace that passes all understanding. This is the blessing Pentecost brings and receives.

The entrance of the Son of God into our flesh in Bethlehem, His entrance into the curse and death of sin, His entrance into the very glory of the Father—these were but the preparatory steps. All these were accomplished so that the word could be fulfilled: "Behold, the tabernacle of God is with men, and He will dwell with them" (Revelation 21:3).

The narrative of the outpouring of the Spirit can be understood only in the light of all that preceded Pentecost. God did not think any sacrifice was too great to make it possible for Him to dwell with sinful men. This is the earthly reflection of Christ's exaltation in heaven, the participation He gives to His friends of the glory He now has with the Father. Let us study what the Spirit is to be to *believers* and the Church, to the *ministers* of the Word and their work, and to the unbelieving *world*.

Power To Preach

Christ promised His disciples that, in the Comforter, He Himself would again come to them. During His life on earth, His personal manifested presence revealed the unseen Father. This was the Father's great gift to men and was the one thing the disciples wanted and needed. Christ entered heaven with this very purpose, that now He might fill the members of His Body with Himself and His glory-life.

When the Holy Spirit came down, He brought what had previously only been a life near the disciples, outside their own. The very Spirit of God's own Son—who had lived and loved, obeyed and died, and was raised and glorified by Almighty power—was now to become their personal life. The Holy Spirit came to be the witness of the wonderful transaction that had taken place in heaven in the placing of their friend and Lord on the throne of heaven. The Spirit came to communicate and maintain this friendship within the disciples as a heavenly reality.

It is indeed no wonder that, as the Holy Spirit came down from the Father through the glorified Son, the disciples' whole nature was filled to overflowing with the joy and power of heaven. They were filled with the presence of Jesus, and their lips overflowed with the praise of the wonderful works of God.

Such was the birth of the Church. Such must be its growth and strength. The most essential element of the true Church after Pentecost is a membership *baptized* with the Holy Spirit and with fire. Every heart was filled with the experience of the presence of the glorified Lord. Every tongue and life witnessed to the wonderful work God had done in raising Jesus to glory and then filling His disciples with that glory.

The baptism of power is not just for preachers, but for every individual member of Christ's body. This will draw the attention of the world and compel confession to the power of Jesus.

In the midst of this joyous praising company of believers, Peter stood up to preach. The story of Pentecost teaches us the true position of the ministry and the secret of its power. A Church full of the Holy Spirit is a power of God to awaken the careless and attract the honest, earnest hearts. It is to such an audience, roused by the testimony of believers, that preaching will come with power. It is out of such a Church of men and women full of the Holy Spirit that Spirit-led preachers will rise up. They will be bold and free to point to every believer as a living witness to the truth of their preaching and the power of their Lord.

Peter's preaching is a most remarkable lesson of what all preaching in the power of the Holy Spirit will be. He preaches Christ from the Scriptures. In contrast with the thoughts of people who had rejected Christ, He sets forth the thoughts of God who had sent Christ. All preaching in the power of the Holy Spirit will be like this.

The Spirit has come for the very purpose of continuing the work Christ began on earth, of making men partakers of His redemption and His life. It could not be otherwise. The Spirit always witnesses of Christ. He did so in the Scriptures. He does so in the believer. The believer's testimony will always be according to Scripture. The Spirit in Christ, the Spirit in Scripture, the Spirit in the Church—as long as this threefold cord is kept intertwined, it cannot be broken.

Power For The Church

The effect of this preaching was marvelous, but not more marvelous than might be expected. The presence and power of Jesus was a reality in the disciples. The power from the throne filled Peter with the sight and experience of Christ exalted at the right hand of God. Power went from him, and his preaching reached its application: "God hath made that same Jesus, whom ye have crucified, both Lord and Christ" (Acts 2:36). Thousands bowed in brokenness of spirit, ready to acknowledge the crucified One as their Lord.

The Spirit came to the disciples and, through them, convinced others of unbelief. The penitent inquirers listen to the command to repent and believe, and they, too, receive the Holy Spirit.

The greater works that Christ had promised to do through the disciples, He has done. In one moment, lifelong prejudice and even bitter hatred gave way to surrender, love, and adoration.

Pentecost is the glorious sunrise of "that day," the first of "those days" of which the prophets and our Lord had so often spoken. Pentecost is the promise and the pledge of what the history of the Church was meant to be.

The Church has not fulfilled her destiny. Even now, after almost two thousand years, she has not risen to the height of her glorious privileges. Even when she strives to accept her calling, to witness for her Lord unto the ends of the earth, she lacks the faith of the Pentecostal Spirit and the possession of His mighty power. Instead of regarding Pentecost as sunrise, the Church often speaks and acts as if it had been noonday, from which the light must begin to lessen. If the Church returns to Pentecost, Pentecost will return to her!

The Spirit of God cannot take possession of

believers beyond their capacity to receive Him. The promise is waiting. The Spirit is now in all His fullness. Our ability to receive needs to be enlarged. Pentecost comes when believers continue with one accord in praise and love and prayer. The Holy Spirit comes when faith holds fast the promise and gazes upon the exalted Lord, in the confidence that He will make Himself known in power in the midst of His people.

Jesus Christ is still Lord of all, crowned with power and glory. His longing to reveal His presence in His disciples, and to make them share the glory-life in which He dwells, is as fresh and full as when He first ascended the throne. Let us take our place at His footstool. Let us yield ourselves in strong, expectant faith, to be filled with the Holy Spirit and to testify for Jesus. Let the indwelling Christ be our life, our strength, and our testimony. From such a Church, Spirit-filled preachers will rise, and the power will go forth making Christ's enemies bow at His feet.

The perfect health of a body means the health of every member. The healthy action of the Spirit in the Church requires the health of every individual believer. Let us pray and labor for this: that the presence of Christ will indwell every believer. May this be our preparation for the united prayer and service which will make our seasons of worship a continuous Pentecost. May we be a waiting, receptive, worshipping Church on earth met by the Spirit of Christ from heaven.

Prayer

Our Father, reveal to Your Church that we are Christ's own Body, sharing with Him in His life, His power, and His glory. Show us how the Holy Spirit, as the bearer of that life and power and glory, is waiting to reveal it within us.

Our Father, in the name of Jesus, revive Your Church. Make every believer a temple full of the Holy Spirit. Make every church a consecrated company that testifies of a present Christ, waiting for the fullness of the power from on high. Make every preacher of the Word a minister of the Spirit. And let Pentecost be the sign throughout the earth that Jesus reigns, that His redeemed are His Body, that His Spirit works, and that every knee will bow to Him. Amen.

Chapter 7

POWER FOR YOUR LIFE

"Ye shall be baptized with the Holy Ghost not many days hence. . . .But ye shall receive power, after that the Holy Ghost is come upon you: and ye shall be witnesses unto me"—Acts 1:5,8.

"Tarry ye in the city. . .until ye be endued with power from on high"—Luke 24:49.

The disciples had heard from John about the baptism of the Spirit. Jesus had spoken to them of the Father's giving of the Spirit to those who ask Him. And on the last night He had spoken of the Spirit dwelling in them, witnessing with them, having come to them to convince the world of sin. This coming of the Holy Spirit was connected in their mind with the work they would have to do and the power for it.

Our Lord summed up all His teaching in the promise, "Ye shall receive power, after the Holy Ghost is come upon you: and ye shall be My witnesses." This must have been what the disciples were looking for: a divine power for the new work of being the witnesses of a crucified and risen

Jesus.

This was in perfect harmony with all they had seen of the Spirit's work in Holy Scripture. In the days before the flood, the Spirit had been striving with men. In the ministry of Moses, the Spirit equipped him and the seventy for the work of ruling and guiding Israel. In the days of the judges, the Spirit gave the power to fight and conquer the enemies. In the times of kings and prophets, He gave boldness to testify against sin and power to proclaim a coming redemption. Every mention of the Spirit in the Old Testament is connected with the Kingdom of God and equipping men to serve in it.

With the great prophecy of the Messiah, the Son of God opened His ministry at Nazareth. His being, anointed with the Spirit, had the one purpose of bringing deliverance to the captives and gladness to the mourners. To the mind of the disciples, as students of the Old Testament and followers of Christ Jesus, the promise of the Spirit had only one meaning—power for the great work they had to do for their Lord when He ascended the throne. The Spirit's work of comforting, teaching, sanctifying the soul, and glorifying Jesus was only a means to an end. The Spirit's chief purpose was their endowment with power for the service of their departed Lord.

Power To Witness

I wish that the Church understood this today! All prayers for the guiding influence of the Holy Spirit in God's people to have this as their aim: power to witness for Christ and do effective service in conquering the world for Him. Waste of power is always cause for regret to those who witness it. The economy of power is one of the important principles in all organizations and industry.

The Spirit is the great power of God. The Holy Spirit is the great power of God's redemption as it comes down from the throne of Christ. Would God waste this power on those who seek it only for their own sake with the desire of being beautifully holy or wise or good? No. The Holy Spirit is the power from on high for carrying on the work for which Jesus sacrificed His throne and His life. The essential condition for receiving that power is that we be found ready and able to do the work the Spirit has come to accomplish.

"My witnesses." These two words contain the most perfect description of the Spirit's work and our work—the work for which nothing less than His divine power is needed, the work for which our weakness is suited. There is nothing as effective as an honest witness. The learned eloquence of a lawyer must pay attention to it. There is nothing as simple as telling what we have seen and heard or witnessing to what has been done in us. It was the great work of Jesus Himself: "To this end was I born, and for this cause came I into the world, that I should bear witness unto the truth" (John 18:37). To make us witnesses of Jesus—that is what the almighty power of the Spirit is needed for, and what He was sent to accomplish. We need the divine power of the heavenly life to quicken the testimony of our lips and life.

The Holy Spirit makes us witnesses because He Himself is a witness. Jesus said that the Spirit witnessed of Him. When Peter, on the day of Pentecost, preached that Christ had poured forth the Holy Spirit, he spoke from experience. The Holy Spirit witnessed to him and in him of the glory of his exalted Lord. It was this witness of the Spirit to the reality of Christ's power and presence that made Peter so bold and strong to speak before the council: "God hath exalted (Him). . .to be a Prince and a Saviour and we are witnesses of these things; and so is the Holy Ghost" (Acts 5:31,6:31,32).

When the Holy Spirit becomes to us a witness to what Jesus is at the present moment in His glory, then our witness will be in His power. We may know all that the Gospels record and all that Scripture teaches of the person and work of Jesus. We may even speak from past experience of what we once knew about the power of Jesus. However, this is not the witness of power that will have an effect on the world. It is the presence of the Spirit witnessing to the personal Jesus that gives our witness that breath of life from heaven. You can truly witness to just as much of Jesus as the Holy Spirit is witnessing to you in life and truth.

The Baptism Of Power

The baptism of power, the endowment of power, is sometimes spoken of and sought after as a special gift. Paul asked very distinctly for the Ephesians, who had been sealed with the Holy Spirit, that the Father would still give them "the Spirit of wisdom" (Ephesians 1:17). Then we cannot be far wrong in praying just as definitely for the "Spirit of power." He who searches the hearts knows what is the mind of the Spirit, and will give, not according to the correctness of our words, but according to the Spirit-breathed desire of our hearts.

Let us examine another of Paul's prayers and plead that God would grant us to be mightily strengthened by His Spirit. "That He would grant you, according to the riches of His glory, to be strengthened with might by His Spirit in the inner man" (Ephesians 3:16). No matter how we formulate our prayers, one thing is certain: The power of the Spirit will come as a result of humble, unceasing prayer. The Spirit is never anything separate from God. In all His going out and working, He is still the innermost self of God. It is God Himself who is mighty to do above what we ask or think and who will in Christ give us to be clothed with the power of the Spirit.

In seeking for this power of the Spirit, let us note *the manner* of His working. There is one mistake we must especially be aware of. It is that of expecting always *to feel* the power when it works. Scripture links power and weakness in a wonderful way, not as succeeding each other, but as existing together. "I was with you in *weakness. . .*and my preaching was. . .in *power*;"

"When I am *weak,* then am I *strong.*" (See 1 Corinthians 2:3-5; 2 Corinthians 4:7,16; 6:10; 12:10; 13:3,4.)

The power is the power of God, given to faith, and faith grows strong in the dark. The Holy Spirit hides himself in the weak things that God has chosen, so that flesh may not glory in His presence. Spiritual power can only be known by the Spirit of faith. The more we acknowledge our weakness, the more confidently we can expect the Spirit's power, even when nothing is felt.

Christians lose much not only by not waiting for the power, but by waiting in the wrong way. Combine ready obedience to every call of duty, no matter how weak you feel, with a dependent waiting and expectation of power from on high. Let intervals of rest and communion be the exercise of prayer and faith in the power of God dwelling in you and waiting to work through you. Then your time of exertion and effort will bring the proof that by faith, out of weakness, we are made strong.

The Condition And Purpose Of Power

Let us also make no mistake about *the condition* of the working of this divine power. The person who wants to command nature must first obey her. We do not need much grace to long and ask for power, even the power of the Spirit. Who would not be glad to have power? Many pray earnestly for power in their work, and do not receive it, because they do not accept the only attitude in which the power can work.

We want to get possession of the power and use it. God wants the power to get possession of us and use us. If we give up ourselves to the power to rule in us, the power will give itself to us, to rule through us. Unconditional submission and obedience to the power in our inner life is the one condition of our being clothed with it.

God gives the Spirit to the obedient. Power belongs to God and remains His forever. If you want His power to work in you, surrender to His guidance even in the least things.

Let us be clear regarding *the purpose* of this power and the work it is to do. Men are very careful to economize power and to store it where it can do its work most effectively. God does not give this power for our own enjoyment. He gives it for one purpose—to glorify His Son. Those who are faithful to this one purpose and prove they are ready at any cost to glorify God will receive the power from on high.

God seeks men and women whom He can clothe with power. The Church is looking for them, wondering at the weakness of so much of its ministry and worship. The world waits to be convinced that God is indeed in the midst of His people. The perishing millions are crying for deliverance, and the power of God is waiting to accomplish it.

Let us not be content with praying for God to visit and to bless the unsaved or with our own efforts to do the best we can for them. Rather, let each believer give himself completely to live as a witness for Jesus. Let us plead with God to show

His people what it means to be Christ's representatives just as He was the Father's representative. Let us believe that the Spirit of power is within us. The Father will, as we wait on Him, fill us with the power of the Spirit.

As the character of a body depends upon the different particles of which it is composed, so the power of the body of Christ will be decided by the state of its individual members. The Holy Spirit cannot work mightily through the Church in the world until the mass of individual believers give themselves completely to their Lord to be filled with His Spirit. Let us labor and pray for this.

Prayer

My Father, I ask You to teach me that I have the power of the living Jesus. I desire that the power be a divine strength in human weakness, so that the glory may be Yours alone. May I learn to receive it in a faith that allows Jesus to hold the power and do the work in the midst of weakness. May Jesus be so present with me that my witness may be of Him alone. I desire to submit my whole being to this divine power. I bow before His rule every day and all day long. I humble myself to do all He commands. Father, let the power of Your Spirit rule in me so that I can be ready to be used. May my one purpose in life be that Your blessed Son receive the honor and the glory. Amen.

Chapter 8

HOW TO WORSHIP IN THE SPIRIT

"The hour cometh, and now is, when the true worshippers shall worship the Father in spirit and in truth: for the Father seeketh such to worship him. God is a Spirit: and they that worship him must worship him in spirit and in truth"—John 4:23,24.

"We are the circumcision, which worship God in the spirit, and rejoice in Christ Jesus, and have no confidence in the flesh"—Philippians 3:3.

Man's highest glory is to worship. He was created for fellowship with God. Worship is the greatest expression of that fellowship. All the exercises of the Christian life—meditation and prayer, love and faith, surrender and obedience—culminate in worship. Recognizing God in His holiness and realizing I am the Father's redeemed child, I present my whole being to God in worship. In worship I offer Him the adoration and the glory which is His due. The truest and fullest and nearest approach to God is worship. Every senti-

worship is man's highest destiny because in it God is all.

Jesus tells us that a new worship would begin with His coming. All that the heathen or the Samaritans called worship, even all that the Jews knew of worship in God's law, would make way for something new—the worship in Spirit and in truth. This is the worship Jesus was to inaugurate by the giving of the Holy Spirit. This now is the only worship which is pleasing to the Father.

We have received the Holy Spirit especially for this worship. The great purpose for which the Holy Spirit is within us is to make us able to worship in Spirit and in truth. "The Father seeketh such to worship Him"—for this He sent forth His Son and His Spirit.

Worship In Spirit

God created man's soul as the seat of his personality and consciousness. His soul was linked through his body with the outer visible world. It was also linked through the spirit with the unseen and the divine. The soul had to decide whether it would yield itself to the spirit and be linked with God and His will, or to be linked to the body and the desires of the flesh.

At the fall of Adam, the soul refused the rule of the spirit and became the slave of the body with its appetites. Man became flesh. The spirit lost its destined place of rule and became little more than a dormant power. It was now a struggling captive instead of the ruling principle. The spirit now stands in opposition to the flesh because of this.

When speaking of the unregenerate man in contrast with the spiritual (1 Corinthians 2:14), Paul calls him physical, soulish, or animal, having only the natural life. The life of the soul understands all our moral and intellectual faculties. Because the soul is under the power of the flesh, man is to be flesh. The body consists of flesh and bone, and the flesh is that part of it which is especially endowed with sensitivity. Through the flesh we receive our sensations from the outer world. It denotes human nature, as it has become subject to the world of sense.

Because the soul has come under the power of the flesh, Scripture speaks of all the attributes of the soul as belonging to the flesh and being under its power. There is a fleshly wisdom and a spiritual wisdom. (See 1 Corinthians 2:12 and Colossians 1:9.) There is service for God that trusts in the flesh and glories in the flesh, and service of God by the spirit. (See Philippians 3:3,4 and Galatians 6:13.) There is a fleshly mind and a spiritual mind. (See Colossians 2:18 and 1:9.) There is a will of the flesh and a will which is of God working by His Spirit. (See John 1:13 and Philippians 2:13.) There is worship which satisfies the flesh, because it is in the power of what flesh can do. (See Colossians 2:18,23.) There is also worship of God which is in the Spirit. Jesus came to make this worship possible and to give a new spirit in our innermost part. Then, within our new spirit, He gives God's Holy Spirit.

True Worship

"In Spirit and in truth." To worship in Spirit is to worship in truth. The words *in Spirit* do not mean to dwell inwardly instead of outwardly. Rather, they mean that which is brought about by God's Spirit, as opposed to man's natural power. So the words *in truth* do not mean hearty, sincere, upright.

When the Old Testament saints worshipped, they knew that God sought truth in the innermost parts. They sought Him with their whole hearts, and yet they did not attain the worship in Spirit and truth which Jesus brought us when He conquered the flesh.

In the Gospel of John, *truth* means the substance, the reality, the actual possession of all that the worship of God implies, both in what it demands and what it promises. John 1:14 speaks of Jesus as "the only begotten of the Father, full of grace and truth." And he adds, "For the law was given by Moses, but grace and truth came by Jesus Christ" (John 1:17).

If we take truth as opposed to falsehood, the law of Moses was just as true as the gospel of Jesus. They both came from God. The law gave only a shadow of "good things to come." (See Hebrews 10:1.) Christ brought us the good things. He was full of truth, because He was Himself *the truth*, the reality, the very life and love and power of God imparting itself to us.

It is easy to see how only worship *in Spirit* can

be worship *in truth*. True worship is the actual enjoyment of that divine power which is Christ's own life and fellowship with the Father, revealed and maintained within us by the Holy Spirit. "The true worshippers shall worship the Father in Spirit and in truth" (John 4:23).

All worshippers are not true worshippers. There may be a great deal of earnest, honest worship without its being worship in Spirit and in truth. The mind may be intensely occupied. The feelings may be deeply moved. The will may be strengthened, yet there may be little of the spiritual worship which stands in the truth of God. There may be great attachment to Bible truth. Yet, because of man's effort, and not the Christ-given, Spirit-breathed worship which God seeks, it is not true worship.

There must be accordance, harmony, and unity between God, who is a Spirit, and the worshippers drawing near in the Spirit. The Father seeks such as these to worship Him. The infinite, perfect Holy Spirit, which God the Father is, must have some reflection in the spirit which is in the believer. This can only be as the Spirit of God dwells in us.

Becoming A True Worshipper

If we strive to become true worshippers, the first thing we need is a sense of the danger that comes from the flesh and its worship. As believers we have in us a double nature—flesh and spirit. The one is the natural part which is always ready to undertake the doing of what is needed in the

69

worship of God. The other is the spiritual part which may still be very weak.

Because of this, we may not yet know how to give the Spirit control. Our mind may delight in the study of God's Word, and our feelings may be moved by the wonderful thoughts revealed there. As we see in Romans 7:22, we may delight in the law of God. Yet, we may be powerless to render that obedience and worship.

We need the Holy Spirit's indwelling for life and worship alike. To receive this we need first of all to have the flesh silenced. "Be silent. . .all flesh, before the Lord" (Zechariah 2:13). "No flesh should glory in His presence" (1 Corinthians 1:29). The Father had already revealed to Peter that Jesus was the Christ. However, when considering what would happen to Jesus on the cross, his mind was not according to the things of God, but the things of men.

Our own spiritual thoughts, and our own efforts to stir up the right feelings within us, must be given up. Our own power to worship must be brought down and laid low, and every approach to God must take place under a very distinct and very quiet surrender to the Holy Spirit.

As we learn how impossible it is to ensure the Spirit's working by our will, we will learn that if we would worship in the Spirit we must walk in the Spirit. Romans 8:9 says, "Ye are not in the flesh, but *in the Spirit*, if so be that the Spirit of God dwell in you." As the Spirit dwells and rules in me, I am in the Spirit and can worship in the

Spirit.

"The hour cometh, and now is, when the true worshippers shall worship the Father in Spirit and in truth; for the Father seeketh such to worship Him." Yes, the Father seeks such worshippers. What He seeks He finds because He Himself accomplishes it. He sent His own Son to seek and to save the lost. He did this to save us and to make us His true worshippers who worship Him in the Spirit.

He then sent the Spirit of His Son, the Spirit of Christ, to be in us. This Spirit is the truth and reality of Christ's actual presence and communicates within us the very life that Christ lived. The hour has come when the true worshippers will worship the Father in Spirit and in truth. The Spirit has been given and dwells within us for this one reason: because the Father seeks such worshippers.

Much worship is, even among believers, not in the Spirit! In private, family, and public worship, many hastily enter into God's presence in the power of the flesh, with little or no waiting for the Spirit to lift us heavenward! It is only the presence and power of the Holy Spirit that equips us for acceptable worship.

The great hindrance to the Spirit is the flesh. The secret of spiritual worship is the death of the flesh. Give it up and in great fear humbly and trustfully wait for the Spirit's life and power to take the place of the life and strength of self.

Prayer

Most Holy God, we confess with shame how much our worship has been in the power and the will of the flesh. We have dishonored You by this, grieved Your Spirit, and brought infinite loss to our own souls. Forgive us and save us from this sin. Teach us never to attempt to worship You except in Spirit and in truth.

Our Father, Your Holy Spirit dwells in us. Strengthen us with power by Him, that our inner man may indeed be a spiritual temple, where spiritual sacrifices are unceasingly offered. Teach us to yield self and the flesh and wait for the Spirit to create in us worship acceptable to You through Christ Jesus. We ask it in the name of Jesus. Amen.

Chapter 9

THE SPIRIT GIVES LIFE

"It is the Spirit that quickeneth; the flesh profiteth nothing: the words that I speak unto you they are spirit, and they are life. . . .Lord, to whom shall we go? thou hast the words of eternal life"—John 6:63,68.

"(God) hath made us able ministers of the new testament; not of the letter, but of the Spirit: for the letter killeth, but the Spirit giveth life"— 2 Corinthians 3:6.

Our blessed Lord spoke of Himself as the bread of life. He spoke of His flesh and blood as the meat and drink of eternal life. Many of His disciples found this difficult to understand. Jesus tells them that it is only with the coming and receiving of the Holy Spirit that His words will become clear to them.

"It is the Spirit that quickeneth." In these words and the corresponding ones of Paul, "the Spirit giveth life," we have the nearest approach to what may be called a definition of the Spirit. (Also see 1 Corinthians 16:45.) In the first place, the Spirit always acts as a life-giving principle. His work in the believer, of sealing, sanctifying, enlightening, and strengthening, is all rooted in this: it is as He is known, honored, waited on, and given a high place as the inner life of the soul, that His other gracious workings can be experienced. These are the fruits of the life. It is in the power of the life within that they can be enjoyed.

"It is the Spirit that quickeneth." Our Lord places the flesh in opposition with the Spirit. He says, "the flesh profiteth nothing." He is not speaking of the flesh as the foundation of sin. He means the *flesh* as the power in which the natural man or the unyielded believer seeks to serve God or to understand spiritual truths. Our Lord indicates the futile efforts of the flesh in the words, "profiteth nothing." These efforts are not sufficient. They cannot reach spiritual reality, the divine things themselves.

Although the dispensation of the law had a certain glory, and Israel's privileges were very great, Paul says in 2 Corinthians 3:10, "Even that which was made glorious had no glory in this respect, by reason of the glory that excelleth." Even when Christ was in the flesh, His words could not achieve the desired effect in His disciples. It could not happen until the Spirit was given, since "it is the Spirit that quickeneth; the flesh profiteth nothing."

Living Seeds

Christ said, "The words that I speak unto you

74

they are spirit and they are life." He wanted to teach the disciples two things. First, that the words are indeed a living seed with a power to germinate, to assert their own vitality, to reveal their meaning, and to prove their divine power in those who receive them and keep them alive in the heart.

Jesus did not want His disciples to be discouraged if they could not understand His words at once. His Words are Spirit and life. They are not meant for the understanding, but for the life. Coming in the power of the Spirit, higher and deeper than all thought, His words enter into the very roots of the life. They themselves have a divine life, working out with divine energy the truth they reveal into the experience of those who receive them.

Christ also wanted the disciples to learn another lesson. As a result of their spiritual character, Christ's words need a spiritual nature to receive them. Seed needs suitable soil. There must be life in the soil as well as in the seed. The Word must be taken into the life. It is not only to be taken into the mind or the emotions or even the will. The center of that life is man's spiritual nature with conscience as its voice. The authority of the Word must be acknowledged there.

But even this is not enough. Conscience dwells in man as a captive amid powers it cannot control. It is the Spirit that comes from God that will make the words of Christ become truth and power in us. This is done by receiving the Word and making it part of our lives. This truth will keep us from expecting to enjoy the teaching of the Spirit without the Word or to master the teaching of the Word without the Spirit.

Common Errors

One error we make is the seeking of the teaching of the Spirit without the Word. In the Holy Trinity, the Word and the Spirit are always in each other, one with the Father. It is the same with the God-inspired words of Scripture. The Holy Spirit has for all ages put the thoughts of God in the written Word. He lives now for this very purpose in our hearts, to reveal the power and the meaning of that Word.

If you want to be full of the Spirit, be full of the Word.

If you want to have the divine life of the Spirit grow strong within you and acquire power in every part of your nature, let the Word of Christ dwell richly in you.

If you want the Spirit to call to your mind and apply at the right moment what Jesus has spoken to your need, have the Words of Christ abiding in you.

If you want the Spirit to reveal to you the will of God in each circumstance of life, have the Word living in you, ready for His use.

If you want the eternal Word as your light, let the written Word be transcribed on your heart by the Holy Spirit. "The words that I speak unto you, they are spirit and they are life." Take them and treasure them. It is through them that the Spirit manifests His quickening power.

Another error is a more common one. Do not think for one moment that the Word can unfold its life in you, unless the Spirit within you accepts and appropriates it in the inner life. The first and main purpose in much of Scripture reading, study, and preaching is to reach the *meaning* of the Word.

People think if they know correctly and exactly what the Word means, then the blessing will come as a natural consequence. This is by no means the case. The Word is a seed. In every seed there is a fleshy part, in which the life is hidden. One may have the most precious and perfect seed in its bodily substance, but unless it is exposed in suitable soil to the influence of sun and moisture, the life will never grow. We may hold the words and the doctrines of Scripture intelligently and earnestly, and yet we may know little of their life or power.

We need to remind ourselves and the Church that the Scriptures, which were spoken by holy men of old as they were moved by the Holy Spirit, can only be understood by holy men as they are taught by the same Spirit. "The words I speak are spirit and life." For the understanding and partaking of them "the flesh profiteth nothing: it is the Spirit that quickeneth," the Spirit of life within us.

This is one of the very solemn lessons which the history of the Jews in the time of Christ teaches us.

They thought they were extremely zealous for God's Word and honor, and yet it turned out that all their zeal was for their human interpretation of God's Word. Jesus said to them, "Search the Scriptures; for in them ye think ye have eternal life: and they are they which testify of Me. And ye will not come to Me, that ye may have life" (John 5:39,40).

They did indeed trust the Scriptures to lead them to eternal life, yet they never saw that the Scriptures testified of Christ, and so they would not come to Him. The Jews studied and accepted Scripture in the light and in the power of their human understanding, and not in the light and power of God's Spirit as their life.

This is also the reason for the weakness in the life of many believers who read and know a great deal of Scripture. They do not know that it is the Spirit that quickens. The human understanding, however intelligent, however earnest, profits nothing. They think that in the Scriptures they have eternal life, but they know little of the living Christ as their life in the power of the Spirit.

Life In The Spirit

The solution is very simple: we must refuse to deal with the written Word without the quickening Spirit. Let us never take Scripture into our hand, mind, or mouth without realizing the need and the promise of the Spirit.

First, in a quiet act of worship, look to God to give and renew the workings of His Spirit within you. Then, in a quiet act of faith, yield yourself to the power that dwells in you. Then wait on Him so that not only the mind, but the life in you, may be opened to receive the Word. The words of Christ are indeed Spirit and life.

Just as the Lord's words are Spirit and life, so the Spirit must be in us as the Spirit of our life. Deeper down than mind, feeling, or will, the very root of all these, and their life-giving principle, must be the Spirit of God. Nothing else can reach the Spirit of life in the words of the living God.

We must wait on the Holy Spirit within us to receive and reveal the words in His quickening power and work them into the very life of our life. We will know in truth what it means: "It is the Spirit that quickeneth." We will see how divinely right it is that the words which are Spirit and life should be met in us by the Spirit and the life dwelling within. They alone will unfold their meaning, impart their substance, and give their divine strength and fullness to the Spirit and the life already within us.

Prayer

Lord God, I thank You again for the wonderful gift of the indwelling Spirit. Father, give me the Spirit of wisdom. May I know how deeply spiritual each word of Yours is, and may I know that spiritual things can only be spiritually discerned. Teach me in all my contact with Your Word to deny the flesh and the fleshly mind and to wait in deep humility and faith for the inward working of the Spirit to quicken the Word. May my meditation of Your Word, my keeping of it in faith and obedience, be in Spirit and in truth, in life and in power. Amen.

Chapter 10

THE SPIRIT OF THE GLORIFIED JESUS

"He that believeth on me, as the scripture hath said, out of his belly shall flow rivers of living water. (But this spake he of the Spirit, which they that believe on him should receive: for the Holy Ghost was not yet given; because that Jesus was not yet glorified)"—John 7:38,39.

Our Lord promises that those who come unto Him and drink, who believe in Him, will not only never thirst, but will themselves become fountains from which streams of living water will flow forth. The apostle John explains that the promise was a prospective one that would have to wait for its fulfillment until the Spirit would be poured out. He also gave the reason for this delay: The Holy Spirit *was not yet* because Jesus *was not yet* glorified.

The expression: the Spirit was not yet has appeared strange, and so the word *given* has been inserted. But the expression, if accepted as it stands, may guide us into the true understanding of the real significance of the Holy Spirit not coming until Jesus was glorified.

We have learned that God has given a twofold revelation of Himself, first as God in the Old Testament, then as Father in the New. We know how the Son, who had from eternity been with the Father, entered upon a new stage of existence when He became flesh. When He returned to heaven, He was still the same only begotten Son of God, and yet not altogether the same. For He was now the first begotten from the dead, clothed with that glorified humanity which He had perfected and sanctified for Himself.

In the same way, the Spirit of God poured out at Pentecost was also something new. Throughout the Old Testament He was always called the Spirit of God or the Spirit of the Lord. He did not yet bear the name of Holy Spirit as His own proper name. It is only in connection with the work He has to do in preparing the way for Christ that the proper name comes into use. (See Luke 1:15,35.)

When poured out at Pentecost, He came as the Spirit of the glorified Jesus, the Spirit of the incarnate, crucified, and exalted Christ. He came to us as the bearer and communicator of the life that had been interwoven into human nature in the person of Christ Jesus. It is in this capacity that He especially bears the name of Holy Spirit, for it is as the indwelling One that God is holy.

As this Spirit dwelt in Jesus in the flesh, and can also dwell in us in the flesh, it is literally true that the Holy Spirit was not yet. The Spirit of the glorified Jesus—the Son of man become the Son of

God—could not be until Jesus was glorified.

The Spirit Of Jesus

This thought further opens up to us the reason why it is not the Spirit of God as such, but the Spirit of Jesus, that could be sent to dwell in us. Sin had not only disturbed our relationship to God's law, but to God Himself. Along with the divine favor, we lost the divine life.

Christ not only came to deliver man from the law and its curse, but to bring human nature itself into the fellowship of the divine life again, in order to make us partakers of the divine nature. He could do this, not by an exercise of divine power on man, but only in free, moral human development.

Having become flesh, He had to sanctify the flesh and make it a suitable and willing receptacle for the indwelling of the Spirit of God. Having done this, He had to bear the curse of sin and to give Himself as the seed to bring forth fruit in us. His nature was glorified in the resurrection, and His Spirit came forth as the Spirit of His human life, glorified into the union with the divine. *By this He made us partakers of all that He had personally acquired.*

In virtue of Christ's atonement, man now had a right and title to the fullness of the divine Spirit as never before. In virtue of His having perfected in Himself a new holy human nature on our behalf, He could now communicate what previously had no existence—a life at once human and divine.

From that point the Spirit, just as He was the personal divine life, could also become the personal life of men. As the Spirit is the personal life-principle in God Himself, He can be the same in the child of God. The Spirit of God's Son can now be the Spirit that cries in our heart, "Abba, Father." Of this Spirit it is most fully true, "The (Spirit) was not yet, because Jesus was not yet glorified."

But now *Jesus has been glorified!* Now that there is the Spirit of the glorified Jesus, the promise can now be fulfilled: "He that believeth on Me. . .out of (him) shall flow rivers of living water." The great transaction which took place when Jesus was glorified is now an eternal reality.

When Christ entered with human nature (in the flesh) into the Holy of Holies, that of which Peter speaks took place: "Being by the right hand of God exalted and having received of the Father the promise of the Holy Ghost" (Acts 2:33). In our place, and on our behalf, as man and the Head of man, Jesus was admitted into the full glory of the divine. His human nature became the receptacle and the dispenser of the divine Spirit.

Then the Holy Spirit could come down as the Spirit of the God-man, Jesus Christ, and yet as truly the spirit of man. He could come down as the Spirit of the glorified Jesus to be in each one who believes in Jesus. He comes as the Spirit of His personal presence, and, at the same time, He comes as the spirit of the personal life of the believer.

The perfect union of God and man had been in Jesus. This union was finally completed when Jesus sat down upon the throne. He entered a new stage of existence, a glory not known before. A new era has now begun in the life and the work of the Spirit. He can now come down to witness of the perfect union of the divine and the human and, in becoming our life, make us partakers of it.

There is *now* the Spirit of the glorified Jesus which has been poured forth. We have received the Spirit of Jesus to stream into us, to stream through us, and to stream forth from us in rivers of blessing.

Christ In Us

The glorifying of Jesus and the streaming forth of His Spirit are intimately connected. The two are inseparably linked. If we want to have this Spirit of the glorified Jesus, we must come to Jesus Himself. We must not simply rest content with the faith that trusts in the cross and its pardon. We must seek to know the new life of divine power in human nature.

The Spirit of the glorified Jesus is the witness and the bearer of this new life. This is the mystery which was hidden from ages and generations, but is now made known by the Holy Spirit: *Christ in us*. He really can live His divine life in us who are in the flesh.

We have an intense, personal interest in knowing what it means that Jesus is glorified. We want to understand how the life and glory of God could be in human nature. This is not only because we will one day see Him in His glory and share in it ourselves, but even now, day by day, we are to live in it. The Holy Spirit is able to be to us just as much as we are willing to have of Him and of the life of the glorified Lord.

"This spake (Jesus) of the Spirit, which they that believe on Him should receive: for the (Spirit) was not yet; because that Jesus was not yet glorified." God be praised! *Jesus has been glorified.* There is now the Spirit of the glorified Jesus.

In the Old Testament only the unity of God was revealed. When the Spirit was mentioned, it was always as His Spirit, the power by which God was working. He was not known on earth as a person. In the New Testament the Trinity is revealed. With Pentecost the Holy Spirit descended as a person to dwell in us.

This is the fruit of Jesus' work—we now have the personal presence of the Holy Spirit on earth. Christ Jesus, the second person, the Son, came to reveal the Father, and the Father dwelt and spoke in Him. In the same way the Spirit, the third person, comes to reveal the Son, and in Him the Son dwells and works in us. This is the glory by which the Father glorified the Son of man, because the Son had glorified Him.

In His name and through Him, the Holy Spirit descends as a person to dwell in believers and to make the glorified Jesus a present reality within them. This is what Jesus means by whoever believes in Him shall never thirst, but shall have rivers of water flowing out of him. This alone satisfies the soul's thirst and makes it a fountain to quicken others.

Faith's Living Water

"He that believeth on Me, out of his belly shall flow rivers of living water." Jesus said this of the Spirit. Here we have once again the key of all God's treasures: *He that believeth on Me.* It is the glorified Jesus who baptizes with the Holy Spirit. Let each person who longs for the full blessing promised here only believe in Him. Let us believe that He is indeed glorified, that all He is and does is in the power of a divine glory.

According to the riches of His glory, God can now work in us. We have the personal presence of the Spirit on earth within us. By faith, the glory of Jesus in heaven and the power of the Spirit in our hearts become inseparably linked. When we are in fellowship with Jesus, the stream will flow ever stronger and fuller, into us and out of us.

Remember that thinking about these things and understanding them cannot constitute believing. *Believing* is that power of the renewed nature which forsakes self and allows the glorified Christ to come and take possession of us. Faith in Jesus makes self humbly realize that the Spirit has now come in to be its leader, its strength, and its life. Faith in Jesus and a quiet surrender before Him assures us that, as we wait on Him, He will cause the river to flow.

Prayer

Blessed Lord Jesus, I do believe. Help my unbelief and perfect the work of faith in me. Teach me that the Holy Spirit and His power is the glory which You give to us. Teach me to hold these blessed truths in my mind, but with my spirit to wait on You to be filled with Your Spirit.

Lord, I bow before Your glory in humble faith. Let all the life of self and the flesh be brought low and perish, as I worship and wait before You. Let the Spirit of glory become my life. Let His presence break down all trust in self and make room for You. Let my life be one of faith in the Son of God, who loved me and gave Himself for me. Amen.

Chapter 11

THE INDWELLING COMFORTER

"I will pray the Father, and he shall give you another Comforter, that he may abide with you for ever; Even the Spirit of truth; whom the world cannot receive, because it seeth him not, neither knoweth him: but ye know him; for he dwelleth with you, and shall be in you"—John 14:16,17.

"He shall be in you." In these simple words, our Lord announces that wonderful mystery of the Spirit's indwelling which was to be the crown of His redeeming work. For this, man was created. Throughout the ages, the Spirit struggled in vain to achieve God's mastery within the heart of men. It was for this that Jesus lived and died. Without this mastery, the Father's purpose and the Spirit's work would fail to accomplish their task.

Jesus hardly mentioned this to the disciples because He knew they would not understand. But on the last night, He disclosed the divine secret that, when He left them, their loss would be compensated by a greater blessing than His bodily presence. Another would come in His place to abide *with* them and to dwell *in* them forever.

The Divine Indwelling

Our Father has given us a twofold revelation of Himself. In His Son, He reveals *His holy image* and invites us to become like Him by receiving Him into our hearts and lives. In His Spirit, He sends forth *His divine power* to enter into us and prepare us from within for receiving the Son and the Father. Before Christ, spiritual life was external and preparatory. There were at times special and mighty workings of the Spirit, but the indwelling of the Spirit was unknown. Man had not yet become a temple of God in the Spirit.

The Spirit is the essence of the personality of the Trinity. Therefore, this Spirit of the divine life is now to be *in us,* in the deepest sense of the word—the essence of our lives, the root of our personalities, the very life of our being. He is to be one with us, dwelling in us, even as the Father in the Son and the Son in the Father.

If we would enter into the full understanding of what our Lord promised here, we must remember that He speaks of a *divine* indwelling. Wherever God dwells, He hides Himself. He hides Himself in nature, but most men do not see Him there. In the Old Testament, He hid Himself in the tabernacle. It was often only after He was gone that they said, "Surely the Lord is in this place; and I knew it not" (Genesis 28:16).

Jesus came to reveal God, yet He came humbly

90

as man without "form or comeliness." Even His own disciples were at times offended by His actions. Men always expect the Kingdom of God to come dramatically and to be visual. They do not know that it is a hidden mystery to be received only as God makes Himself known in hearts that are surrendered and prepared for Him.

Christians are always ready, when the promise of the Spirit is presented, to form some idea about how His leading can be known in their thoughts. They wonder how His quickening will affect their feelings, how His power will change their will and conduct. They need to be reminded that the Spirit operates deeper than the soul where mind, feeling, and will originate. It is in the depths of the spirit that the Holy Spirit comes to dwell.

Allowing God To Work

This indwelling is first of all recognized by faith. Even when I cannot see the least evidence of His working, I am quietly to believe that He dwells in me. By faith I am to trustfully count upon His working and to wait for it. In that faith I must deny my own wisdom and depend upon Him to work with complete trust. His first workings may be so hidden that I can hardly recognize them as coming from Him. They may appear to be nothing more than the voice of conscience or the familiar sound of some Bible truth.

This is the time for faith to believe the Master's promise and to trust that the Spirit is within me and will guide me. By faith I can continually yield up my whole being to His rule and mastery. In faithfulness my soul will be prepared for knowing His voice better. Out of the hidden depths, His power will move to take possession of mind and will, and the indwelling in the hidden recesses of my heart will grow into a being filled with His fullness.

Faith is the one faculty of our spiritual nature by which we can recognize the divine in whatever unlikely appearances it clothes itself. If this is true of the Father in His glory as God, and the Son as the manifestation of the Father, how much more must it be true of the Spirit. The unseen divine life-power comes to clothe Himself, and hide Himself away, within our weakness.

The deep importance of the indwelling of the Spirit is evident from the place it occupies in our Lord's parting words. Before ascending to the Father, He speaks of the Spirit as teacher, as witness, as representing Himself, and as convincing the world. It is of little value that we know all that the Spirit can do for us unless we put first what the Master gave first place, *the indwelling Spirit* is to be our teacher and our strength.

The Spirit's Dwelling Place

In writing to the Corinthians, Paul had to reprove them for their terrible sins. Yet, he says to all, including the weakest and most unfaithful believer, "Know ye not that ye are the temple of God, and that the Spirit of God dwelleth in you?" (1 Corinthians 3:16). Paul knows that if this truth were given the place God meant it to have, it would be the motive and the power to live a new and holy life.

To the backsliding Galatians, Paul pleads that they have already *received* the Spirit by the preaching of faith. God had sent forth the Spirit of His Son *into their hearts*. They had life by the Spirit in them. If they could only understand and believe this, they would also walk in the Spirit.

It is this teaching the Church of Christ needs in our day. I am deeply persuaded that many believers are ignorant of this aspect of the truth concerning the Holy Spirit. This is the cause of their failure to have a holy walk with the Lord. Many Christians pray for the Holy Spirit's power and confess their entire and absolute dependence on Him. However, unless His personal, continual, divine indwelling is acknowledged and experienced, failure will continue.

The Holy Spirit wants His resting place free from all intrusion and disturbance. God wants entire possession of His temple. Jesus wants His home all to Himself. He cannot do His work there, He cannot rule and reveal Himself, unless the home, the inner being, is possessed and filled by the Holy Spirit.

Prayer

Lord Jesus, You have sent forth Your Holy Spirit into our hearts to be the power that lives and acts in our innermost being and to give us the revelation of Yourself. Bring Your Church to see this truth that has been so hidden and lost, to experience it, and to bear witness to it in power.

May every true believer have the indwelling and the leading of Your Spirit. Teach me, my Lord, to wait on You, as by Your Spirit You work within me. May I constantly be aware that Christ's Spirit dwells in me. Amen.

Chapter 12

HOW TO KNOW THE SPIRIT

"The Spirit of truth; whom the world cannot receive, because it seeth him not, neither knoweth him: but ye know him; for he dwelleth with you, and shall be in you"—John 14:17.

"Know ye not that ye are the temple of God, and that the Spirit of God dwelleth in you?"—1 Corinthians 3:16.

The value of true spiritual knowledge in the Christian life is very important. A man whose inheritance comes to him is no richer if he does not know how to take possession of it. In the same way, the gifts of God's grace cannot bring their full blessing until we truly understand and possess them.

In Christ are *hid* all the treasures of wisdom and knowledge. It is the *knowledge* of Christ Jesus for which the believer is willing to count all things but loss. It is because of the lack of true knowledge of what God in Christ has prepared for us that the lives of believers are so weak.

Paul prayed for the Ephesians—that the Father

would give them *the Spirit of wisdom* and revelation in the *knowledge* of Him that they might *know* the hope of their calling and the riches of the inheritance and the exceeding goodness of the power working in them (1:17-19). This is a prayer we can never pray enough, whether for ourselves or for others.

But it is important that we know the teacher through whom all the other knowledge is to come! The Father has given each one of His children not only Christ, who is the Truth, but the Holy Spirit, who is the very Spirit of Christ and the truth. "We have received. . .the Spirit which is of God; that we might know the things that are freely given to us of God" (1 Corinthians 2:12).

Recognizing The Spirit

How do we know when it is the Spirit that is teaching us? If our knowledge of spiritual things is to be to us a certainty and a comfort, we must know the teacher Himself. Knowing Him will be to us the evidence that our spiritual knowledge is no deception. Our blessed Lord assures us that we will *know* the Spirit. Messengers and witnesses do not speak of themselves.

The Holy Spirit, when He testifies of Christ and glorifies Him, must be known and acknowledged. In this way we can have the assurance that the knowledge we receive is indeed of God and not what our human reason has gathered from the Word of God. To know the King's seal is the only safeguard against a counterfeit image. To know the

Spirit is the divine foundation of certainty.

How can the Spirit be known? Jesus says: "Ye know Him, for He dwelleth with you, and shall be in you." The indwelling of the Spirit is the condition of knowing Him. As we allow Him to dwell in us, and allow Him to testify of Jesus as Lord, He will prove Himself to be the Spirit of God. "It is the Spirit that beareth witness, because the Spirit is truth" (1 John 5:6).

The presence of the Spirit as the indwelling teacher of every believer is little known and recognized in the Church. As the result, the workings of the Spirit are few. There is much doubt and hesitation about the recognition of the witness of the Spirit. As the truth and experience of the indwelling of the Spirit are restored among God's people, and the Spirit is free again to work in power among us, His blessed presence will be sufficient proof. We will indeed know Him. "Ye know Him, for He shall be in you."

But as long as His presence is so little recognized, and His power hindered, how is He to be known? If you honestly desire to know that you have the Spirit as a personal possession and teacher, study the teaching of the Word concerning the Spirit. Do not be content with the teachings of men about the Spirit, but go to the Word. Do not be content with your ordinary reading of the Word, or what you already know about its doctrines.

If you earnestly want to know the Spirit, go and search the Word as one thirsting to drink deeply of the water of life. Collect all the scriptures concerning the Spirit, His indwelling and His work, and hide them in your heart. Be determined to accept nothing except what the Word teaches, but accept it heartily. Study the Word in dependence on the Spirit's teaching. If you study it with your human wisdom, your study of it may only confirm your mistaken views.

If you are a child of God, you have the Holy Spirit to teach you, even though you do not yet know how He works in you. Ask the Father to work through Him in you and to make the Word life and light in you. If you submit heartily to the Word, you will find the promise surely fulfilled: you will be taught by God. Give up all your thoughts and man's thoughts as you accept the Word. Ask God to reveal in you, by His Spirit, His thoughts concerning His Spirit. He will surely do so.

The Evidence Of The Spirit

Obedience is the evidence of the Spirit's presence in your life. Jesus gave Him as our teacher and guide. All Scripture speaks of His work as demanding the surrender of the whole life. "If ye through the Spirit do *mortify the deeds of the body,* ye shall live. For as many as *are led* by the Spirit of God, they are the sons of God" (Romans 8:13,14). "Your body is the temple of the Holy Ghost. . .therefore glorify God in your body" (1 Corinthians 6:19,20). "If we live in the Spirit, let us also walk in the Spirit" (Galatians 5:25). "(We) are changed into the same image. . .even as by the Spirit of the Lord'' (2 Corinthians 3:18). Words like these define very distinctly the operations of the Spirit.

God is first known by His works, and so is the Spirit. He reveals God's will and calls us to follow Him in it. As the believer surrenders himself to a life in the Spirit and consents to the rule of Christ, he will find and know the Spirit working in him. It is as we simply make the aim of the Holy Spirit our aim that we are prepared to know Him as dwelling in us. The Spirit Himself will lead us to obey God even as Christ did. We will know the Spirit intimately as we yield ourselves to an obedient life.

Faith has always to do with the invisible, with what appears to man most unlikely. When the divine appeared in Jesus, it was hidden in a lowly form! Thirty years He lived in Nazareth, and they had seen nothing in Him but the son of a carpenter. It was only with His baptism that His divine Sonship came into complete and perfect recognition. Even to His disciples His divine glory was often hidden. When the life of God enters the depths of our sinful being, it will take even more faith to recognize it!

Cultivate the habit of bowing reverently in silence before God to give the Spirit the recognition that is due Him. Wait on the Spirit in deep dependence. Have a season of quiet meditation. In spite of how little we see or feel, let us believe. The divine is always first known by believing. As we continue to believe, we will be prepared to know and to see.

There is no way of knowing a fruit except by tasting it. There is no way of knowing the light except by being in it and using it. There is no way of knowing a person except by conversation with him. There is no way of knowing the Holy Spirit except by possessing Him and being possessed of Him. To live in the Spirit is the only way to know the Spirit. To have Him in us, doing His work and giving us His fellowship, is the path the Master opens when He says: "Ye know Him. . .for He shall be in you."

Believer, for the excellency of the knowledge of Christ Jesus, Paul counted all things but loss. Should we not give up everything to know the glorified Christ through the Spirit? The Father has sent the Spirit so that we may fully share in the glorified Christ! Let us yield ourselves completely to the indwelling and teaching of the blessed Spirit whom the Son has given us from the Father.

Prayer

Blessed Father, may I know Your Holy Spirit by having Him within me. May His witness to Jesus be divinely clear and mighty in my life. May His leading and sanctifying be in holy power. May His indwelling in my spirit be in such truth and life that the consciousness of Him as my life may be as sure as my natural life. Lord God, teach me and all Your people to know Your Spirit—to know that He is in us, to know Him as He reveals the Son and glorifies You as our Father. Amen.

Chapter 13

TRUTH TO LIVE BY

"But when the Comforter is come, whom I will send unto you from the Father, even the Spirit of truth, which proceedeth from the Father, he shall testify of me"—John 15:26.

"When he, the Spirit of truth, is come, he will guide you into all truth: for he shall not speak of himself; but whatsoever he shall hear, that shall he speak"—John 16:13.

God created man in His image—to become like Himself, capable of holding fellowship with Him in His glory. In the Garden two ways were presented to man for attaining this likeness to God. These were typified by the two trees—that of life and that of knowledge. God's way was the former—through life the knowledge and likeness of God would come.

By abiding in God's will and partaking of God's life, man would be perfected. In recommending the other, Satan assured man that knowledge was the one thing to be desired to make us like God. When man chose the light of knowledge above the life of obedience, he entered the terrible path that leads to death. The desire to know became his greatest temptation. His whole nature was corrupted, and knowledge was to him more than obedience and more than life.

Under the power of this deceit that promises happiness in knowledge, the human race is still led astray. This lie shows its power most terribly in connection with God's own revelation of Himself. Even when the Word of God is accepted, the wisdom of the world and of the flesh always enters in. Even spiritual truth is robbed of its power when held, not in the life of the Spirit, but in the wisdom of man. When truth enters into our heart, it becomes the life of the Spirit.

But it may also only reach the outer parts of the soul, the intellect, and the reason. It occupies and pleases our minds and satisfies us with the imagination that it will exercise its influence. However, its power is nothing more than that of human argument and wisdom that never reaches to the true life of the spirit.

There is a truth of the understanding and feelings which is only the human image, the shadow, of divine truth. There is a truth which is substance and reality, communicating the life of the things of which others only think and speak. The truth in shadow, in form, and in thought was all the Jewish law could give. The truth of substance, the truth as a divine life, was what Jesus brought as the only-begotten Son, full of grace and truth. He is Himself "the truth."

In promising the Holy Spirit to His disciples, our Lord speaks of Him as the Spirit of truth. He Himself is that truth and grace and life which He brought from heaven as a spiritual reality to communicate to us. This truth has its existence in the Spirit of God. He is the Spirit, the inner life of that divine truth. And when we receive Him and give up everything to Him, He makes Christ and the life of God real in us.

In His teaching and guiding into the truth, the Spirit does not give us only words and thoughts from a book or a teacher outside of us. Instead, the Spirit enters the secret roots of our lives, plants the truth of God there as a seed, and dwells in it as divine life. When this hidden life is nourished by faith, He strengthens it. Then, it grows stronger and spreads its branches throughout our whole being. Not from without but from within, not in word but in power, in life and truth, the Spirit reveals Christ and all He has for us. Christ, who has been only a Savior outside and above us, becomes truth within us. The Spirit brings the truth into us with His incoming. And then, having possessed us from within, He guides us into all the truth.

In His promise to send the Spirit of truth from the Father, our Lord very definitely tells us what His principal work would be. "He shall bear witness of Me." He had just before said, "I am. . .the truth" (John 14:6). The work of the Spirit of truth is to reveal and impart the fullness of grace and truth that there is in Christ Jesus. He came down from the glorified Lord in heaven to bear witness within us and through us, of the reality and the power of the redemption which Christ has accomplished there.

There are Christians who are afraid that to think much of the Spirit's presence within us will lead us away from the Savior. Looking within ourselves may do this. However, we can be sure that the recognition of the Spirit within us will lead to a fuller spiritual understanding that Christ alone is indeed all in all. He will make our knowledge of Christ—life and truth.

The Teachable Spirit

Note the remarkable words our Lord uses concerning the Spirit: "He will guide you into all truth: for He shall not speak of Himself; but whatsoever He shall hear, that shall He speak." The mark of this Spirit of truth is a divine teachableness. In the mystery of the Holy Trinity, there is nothing more beautiful than this. With a divine equality on the part of the Son and the Spirit, there is also a perfect subordination.

The Son could demand that men honor Him even as they honored the Father, and yet He said, "The Son can do nothing of Himself." We would think He would surely speak His own thoughts. But He speaks only what He hears, and He does only what He sees the Father do: "for what things soever He doeth, these also doeth the Son likewise" (John 5:19). In the same way, the Holy Spirit never speaks from Himself. The Spirit that fears to speak its own words, and only speaks when God speaks, is the Spirit of truth.

This is the kind of attitude He creates and the life He breathes in those who truly receive Him. It is that gentle teachableness which marks the poor in spirit, the broken in heart, who have become conscious that their wisdom is as worthless as their righteousness. Thus they need Christ and the Spirit within them to be the Spirit of truth. He shows us how lacking we are in that waiting, submissive spirit to which alone spiritual meaning can be revealed.

The Spirit opens our eyes to the reason why so much Bible reading, Bible knowledge, and Bible preaching has little fruit unto true holiness. It is because the Bible is studied with a wisdom that is not from above. God was not waited upon nor was wisdom asked for. The mark of the Spirit of truth was lacking. The Spirit of truth is silent. He does not speak unless and until He hears from God in heaven.

These thoughts suggest to us the great danger of the Christian life—seeking to know the truth of God in His Word without the distinct waiting on the Spirit of truth in the heart. Satan still moves among men. Knowledge is still his great temptation. There are many Christians who would confess that their knowledge of divine truth does little for them. It leaves them powerless against the world and sin.

They know little about the light, the liberty, the strength, the joy, and the truth it was meant to bring. This is because they take God's truth to themselves using human wisdom and human thought. They do not wait for the Spirit of truth to lead them into truth. Earnest efforts to abide in Christ and to walk like Christ have failed because their faith was more in the wisdom of man than in the power of God.

Surrendering To God's Lead

Jesus said, "If any man will come after Me, let him deny himself. . .and follow Me" (Matthew 16:24). Many follow Jesus without denying themselves. There is nothing that needs more denying than our own wisdom, the energy of the fleshly mind, as it exerts itself in the things of God. In all our communication with God, in His Word or prayer, in every act of worship, our first step should be a solemn act of surrender. We must deny our power to understand God's Word or to speak our words to Him without the special divine leading of the Holy Spirit. Christians need to deny even more than our own righteousness. Denying our own wisdom is often the most difficult part of the denial of self.

In all worship we need to realize the sole sufficiency and the absolute necessity, not only of the blood, but of the Spirit of Jesus. This is the meaning of the call to be silent unto God to wait on Him. Be quiet in God's presence. In deep humility and stillness, wait and listen and hear what God will say. The Spirit of truth never speaks from Himself. What He hears, that He speaks. A lowly, listening, teachable spirit is the mark of the presence of the Spirit of truth in a life.

The Spirit of truth does not speak at once in thoughts that we can understand and express. These are only skimming the surface. To be true thoughts, they must be deeply rooted. They must have hidden depth in themselves. The Holy Spirit is the Spirit of truth because He is the Spirit of life. The life is the light. He does not speak to thought or feeling in the first place, but to the spirit of man which is within him—in the innermost parts of his heart.

Prayer

Lord, I ask that the Spirit witness to me of Christ Jesus. May the truth of His atonement and blood dwell in me and I in it. May His life and glory be truth in me, a living experience of His presence and power. My Father, may the Spirit of Your Son be my life. May each word of Your Son through Him be made true in me. I thank You once again, my Father, that the Spirit dwells within me. Grant that He may work mightily in me. May all Your people know their privilege and rejoice that the Holy Spirit within them reveals Christ as truth in them. Amen.

Chapter 14

THE GIFT OF THE SPIRIT

"I tell you the truth; It is expedient for you that I go away: for if I go not away, the Comforter will not come unto you; but if I depart I will send him unto you"—John 16:7.

As the Lord left this world, He promised the disciples that His departure would be their gain. The Comforter would take His place and be to them far better than Jesus ever had been or could be in His bodily presence. This is very special in two ways. The Lord's conversation with them had never been broken, but could be interrupted. Now it would even be broken off by death, and they would see Him no more. However, the Spirit would *abide* with them forever. The Spirit would be *in them*. His coming would be as an indwelling presence in which they would have Jesus in them as their life and their strength.

During the life of our Lord on earth, He dealt with each of His disciples according to their individual character and the special circumstances in which they were placed. The conversation was an intensely personal one—in everything He proved that He knew His sheep by name. For each person there was a thoughtful word of wisdom that met each need. Would the Spirit supply this need, too, and provide that tender personal interest and that special individual attention which made the guidance of Jesus so precious?

All that Christ had been to His disciples, the Spirit was to restore in greater power in a relationship that would not be interrupted. They were to be happier, safer, and stronger with Jesus in heaven than they ever could have been with Him on earth. Jesus had been wise and patient to give each disciple what he needed and to make each one feel that Jesus was his best friend. The joy of this kind of relationship could not be terminated. The indwelling of the Spirit was given to restore Christ's very personal friendship and guidance with His disciples and all believers.

Some Christians have great difficulty believing this, much less experiencing it. The thought of Christ as a man walking with people on earth, teaching and guiding them, seems so clear. However, the thought of the Spirit hiding Himself within us, and speaking in the secret depths of our heart, makes His guidance appear much more difficult.

Becoming A Mature Christian

Actually, what seems to be the greater difficulty of this new spiritual communication and guidance is what gives it greater worth. This is the same principle we see in daily life. Difficulty summons our powers, strengthens our will, develops our character, and makes the person.

In a child's first lessons, he has to be helped and encouraged. As he goes on to more difficult ones, the teacher leaves him to his own resources. A youth leaves his parents' house to have the principles that have been instilled in him tested and strengthened. In each case it is expedient that outside help be withdrawn, and the child depend upon himself to apply and assimilate the lessons he has been taught.

God wants to bring us to mature adulthood, not ruled by an outside law, but by the inner life. As long as Jesus was with His disciples on earth, He had to work from the outside in. Yet, He could never effectually reach or master the innermost parts. When He went away, He sent the Spirit to be in the disciples so that their growth would be from within. Taking possession first of the innermost secret recesses of their life by His Spirit, Jesus would have them become what He Himself is, through His Spirit in them. The framing of their lives and the forming of their character would be in the power of the divine Spirit, who really had become their spirit. So they would grow like Jesus—a true, separate person, having life in Himself, and yet only living in the Father.

As long as the Christian only asks what is easy and pleasant, he will never understand that it is better for us that Christ is not bodily on earth. Put aside fear of difficulty and sacrifice as you desire to become a godly person, bearing the full image of the firstborn Son. In all things live in a way pleasing to the Father. The thought that His Spirit may now become our very own will be welcomed with gladness and gratitude.

To follow the leading of the Spirit and especially the personal friendship and guidance of Jesus is much more difficult and dangerous than it would have been to follow Him on earth. However, the privilege we enjoy, the nobility we attain, the intimacy of fellowship with God—all these are infinitely greater.

The Holy Spirit of God comes through the human nature of our Lord, enters into our spirits, and identifies Himself with us. His Spirit becomes our very own just as He was the Spirit of Christ Jesus on earth—surely this is a joy worth any sacrifice, for it is the beginning of the indwelling of God Himself.

Faith In The Invisible

To see that it is such a privilege and to earnestly desire the Spirit does not remove the difficulty. How can the loving personal relationship of Jesus with His disciples on earth be ours now that He is absent and the Spirit is our guide? The answer is faith. With Jesus on earth, the disciples, once they had believed, walked by sight. We walk by faith.

In faith we must accept and rejoice in the word of Jesus: "It is expedient for you that I go away." We must take time to believe it and to rejoice that He has gone to the Father. We must learn to thank and praise Him for calling us to this life in the Spirit. We must believe that in this gift of the Spirit, the presence and communication of our Lord are secured for us. We may not yet understand this because we have failed to believe and rejoice in the gift of the Holy Spirit. By faith we must believe that the Holy Spirit will teach us how this relationship can be enjoyed.

Beware of misunderstanding these words: *will teach us.* We always connect teaching with thoughts. We want the Spirit to suggest to us certain ideas of how Jesus will be with us and in us. This is not what He does. The Spirit does not dwell in the mind, but in the life. The Spirit begins His work not in what *we know,* but in what *we are.* Do not expect to immediately attain a clear understanding of this divine truth.

Knowledge, thought, feeling, and action are all part of that external religion which the external presence of Jesus had also wrought in the disciples. The Spirit was now to be the hidden presence of Jesus within the depths of their personality. The divine life was in newness of power to become their life. And the teaching of the Spirit would begin, not in word or thought, but in *power*—in the power of a life working in them secretly.

It was the power of a faith that knew Jesus was taking charge of their life. The Spirit would inspire them with the faith of the indwelling of His teaching. They would have the life of Jesus within them, and they would by faith know that it was Jesus. Their faith would be the cause and effect of the presence of the Lord in the Spirit.

It is to the person who has such faith that the presence of Jesus becomes as real and all-sufficient as when He was on earth. Why then do believers who have the Spirit not experience His presence more consciously and fully? The answer is very simple: they do not know the Spirit who is within them. They have much faith in Jesus who died, or who reigns in heaven, but little faith in Jesus who dwells in them by His Spirit.

It is this we need: faith in Jesus as the fulfiller of the promise, "He that believeth in Me, out of his belly shall flow rivers of living water" (John 7:38). We must believe that the Holy Spirit is within us as the presence of our Lord Jesus. We must believe this with the faith of understanding that tries to persuade itself of the truth of what Christ says.

Jesus taught that the Holy Spirit was to enforce the words: "The kingdom of God is within you" (Luke 17:21). If we want to have true faith, let us very gently and humbly yield to the Holy Spirit to do His work in us.

Dying To Self

The will and wisdom of man hinders the Holy Spirit. We are still surrounded by a life of self, of the flesh. In the service of God, even in the effort to exercise faith, self is always putting itself forward and exerting its own strength. Every thought, however good, in which our mind runs before the

114

Spirit, must be brought into captivity.

Our own wisdom must be laid captive at the feet of Jesus. As we bring our fleshly activity into subjection and wait on Him, He will not put us to shame, but do His work within us. The Spirit will strengthen our inner life and quicken our faith. He will reveal Jesus. We will learn that the presence and personal guidance of Jesus is ours just as sweetly and mightily as if He were with us on earth.

Prayer

Blessed Lord Jesus, I do rejoice that I can have a fellowship more real, more near, more tender, more effectual than if You were still here on earth. I thank You that Your Holy Spirit dwells within me and helps me to know what that fellowship is. Teach me in the fullness of faith to believe in You from whom the fresh anointing flows and fills my life. Grant that the Church may be awakened to know that the Spirit's indwelling is the secret of her enjoyment of Your presence and the power for fulfilling her calling. May Your abiding presence be my keeper and guide and friend. Amen.

Chapter 15

HOW TO GLORIFY CHRIST

"It is expedient for you that I go away: for if I go not away, the Comforter will not come unto you; but if I depart I will send him unto you. . . .He shall glorify me: for he shall receive of mine, and shall shew it unto you"—John 16:7,14.

Scripture speaks of a twofold glorifying of the Son. The one is by the Father, the other by the Spirit. The one takes place in heaven, the other here on earth. By the one He is glorified "in God Himself;" by the other, "in us" (John 13:32; 17:10). Of the former Jesus spoke: "If God be glorified in Him (the Son of Man), God shall also glorify Him in Himself, and shall straightway glorify Him" (John 13:32). And again, in the high-priestly prayer, "Father, the hour is come; glorify Thy Son. . . .And now, O Father, glorify Me with Thine own self" (John 17:1,5). Of the latter He said: "(The Spirit) shall glorify Me" (John 16:14).

To glorify is to manifest the hidden excellence and worth of an object. Jesus, the Son of Man, was to be glorified when His human nature was admitted to the full participation of the power and glory in which God dwells. He entered into the perfect spirit-life of the heavenly world. All the angels worshipped Him as the Lamb on the throne. The human mind cannot conceive or understand this heavenly, spiritual glory of Christ.

It can only be truly known by being experienced, by being communicated and participated in the inner life. This is the work of the Holy Spirit. He reveals the glory of Christ in us by dwelling and working in us in the life and the power of that glory in which Christ dwells.

The Holy Spirit makes Christ glorious to us and in us. The Son does not seek His own glory. The Father glorifies Him in heaven. The Spirit glorifies Him in our hearts.

Knowing Christ After The Flesh

Before this glorifying of Christ by the Spirit could take place, He first had to go away from His disciples. They could not have Him in the flesh and in the Spirit, too. His bodily presence would hinder the spiritual indwelling. They must part with Him before they could receive the indwelling Christ glorified by the Holy Spirit. Christ Himself had to give up the life He had before He could be glorified in heaven or in us. We must also give up the Christ we have known, if we are indeed to have Him glorified to us and in us by the Holy Spirit.

I am persuaded that this is the point at which

very many of God's dear children need the teaching, "It is expedient that I go away." Like His disciples, they have believed in Jesus. They love and obey Him. They have experienced much of the inexpressible blessedness of knowing and following Him. Yet, they feel that the rest and joy, the light and the power of His abiding indwelling, is not yet theirs.

The influence of the fellowship of other Christians and the teaching of God's ministers has helped and wonderfully blessed them. Christ has become very precious. Yet, they feel something is missing—promises not perfectly fulfilled, desires not fully satisfied.

The only reason can be this: they have not yet fully inherited the promise of the Holy Spirit's living in us. They do not fully understand the expediency of Christ's going away to come again glorified in the Spirit. They have not yet been able to say, "Though we have known Christ after the flesh, yet now henceforth know we Him no more" (2 Corinthians 5:16).

Knowing Christ after the flesh must come to an end and must make way for knowing Him in the power of the Spirit. *After the flesh* means doing things in the power of external influences—of words and thoughts, of efforts and feelings.

The believer who has received the Holy Spirit but does not fully know what this implies does not surrender entirely to His indwelling and leadings. To a great extent, he still has confidence in the flesh. Admitting that he can do nothing without the Spirit, he still labors and struggles in vain to believe and live as he knows he should. He confesses most heartily, and at times experiences most blessedly that Christ alone is his life and strength.

However, it grieves and almost wearies him to think how often he fails to continue in an attitude of trustful dependence in Christ. He tries to believe all there is to be believed of Christ's nearness and keeping and indwelling, and yet, somehow, there are still breaks and interruptions. It is as if faith is not what it should be—the substance of the things hoped for.

The reason must be that his faith itself was still too much the work of the mind, in the power of the flesh, in the wisdom of man. There has indeed been a revelation of Christ as the faithful keeper and the abiding friend. However, that revelation has been taken hold of by the flesh and the fleshly mind. This has made it powerless.

The doctrine of the indwelling Christ has been received into the mixed life, partly flesh and partly spirit. Only the Spirit can glorify Christ. We must give up and cast aside the old way of knowing and believing and having Christ. We must know Christ no more after the flesh. "(The Spirit) shall glorify Me."

The Glory Of Christ

But what does it mean that the Spirit glorifies Christ? What is this glory of Christ that He reveals, and how does He do it? We learn from Scripture what the glory of Christ is. Hebrews 2:8,9 says,

"We see not yet all things put under Him. But we see Jesus. . .crowned with glory and honour." To Him all things have been made subject.

So our Lord connects His being glorified with all things being given to Him. "All Mine are Thine, and Thine are Mine; and I am glorified in them" (John 17:10). In exalting Him above all rule and power and dominion, the Father has put all things in subjection under His feet. "God also hath. . .given Him a name which is above every name: That at the name of Jesus every knee should bow" (Philippians 2:9,10).

The *Kingdom* and the *power* and the *glory* are all one. Unto Him that sitteth on the throne, and to the Lamb in the midst of the throne, be the glory and the dominion forever. It is by His sitting on the throne of the divine glory with all things put in subjection under His feet that we know Jesus has been glorified in heaven. (See Ephesians 1:20-22.)

When the Holy Spirit glorifies Jesus in us, He reveals Him to us in His glory. He takes of the things of Christ and declares them to us. He does not give us just a thought or an image or a vision of that glory in heaven. Instead, He shows it to us as a personal experience and possession. He makes us partake of it in our innermost life. He shows Christ as present in us. All the true, living knowledge we have of Christ is through the Spirit of God.

However, this may exist, even as in the disciples, along with much confusion and failure. But when the Holy Spirit does His perfect work, and reveals the glorified Lord, the throne of His glory is set up in the heart, and He rules over every enemy. Every power is brought into subjection, every thought into captivity to the obedience of Christ. Throughout our renewed nature there rises the song, "Glory to Him that sitteth on the throne." The holy presence of Christ as ruler and governor so fills the heart and life that His dominion rules over all. Sin has no dominion. The law of the Spirit of the life in Christ Jesus has made us free from the law of sin and death.

Removing The Veil

The history of the Church, as a whole, repeats itself in each individual. When the fullness of time is come and faith is perfected, the Spirit of the glorified One enters in power, and Christ dwells in the heart. Yes, the history of Christ Himself repeats itself in the soul.

In the temple were two holy places—the one before the veil, the other within the veil, or the Most Holy. In His earthly life, Christ dwelt and ministered in the Holy Place outside the veil. The veil of the flesh kept Him out of the Most Holy. When the veil of the flesh was torn, He could enter the inner sanctuary of the full glory of the Spirit-life in heaven.

The believer, who longs to have Jesus glorified within by the Spirit, must learn that there is something better. In him the veil of the flesh must also be torn. He must enter into this special part of Christ's work through the new and living way into

122

the Holiest of All.

Then, the soul sees how completely Jesus has triumphed over the flesh and entered with His flesh into the Spirit-life. The soul sees how perfect His power is over everything in our flesh that could hinder us. The soul sees how perfect the entrance and the indwelling of Jesus as keeper and King can be in the power of the Spirit. The veil is taken away, and the life in the holy place is now one in the Spirit, in the full presence of the glory.

This tearing of the veil, this enthronement of Jesus as the glorified One in the heart, is not always with the sound of trumpet and shouting. At times it may be that way for some, but in others it takes place amid the deep trembling of a stillness where a sound is not heard. Zion's King still comes meek and lowly with the Kingdom to the poor in spirit. Without form or comeliness He enters in, and the Holy Spirit glorifies Him to the one whose faith does not see but believes. The eye of flesh did not see Him on the throne.

To the world it was a mystery. Just when all within us appears weak and empty, the Spirit secretly brings the divine assurance and experience that Christ the glorified One has taken up His abode within us. The soul knows, in silent worship and adoration, that Jesus is master and that His throne in the heart is established in righteousness. The promise is now fulfilled: "(The Spirit) shall glorify Me."

Prayer

Lord Jesus, teach us to maintain our closeness to You. Make our heart and life Yours alone. Teach us to hold fast our confidence that the Spirit who is within us will perfect His work. Above all, teach us to yield ourselves in ever-increasing dependence and emptiness to wait for the Spirit's teaching and leading. We desire to have no confidence in the flesh, its wisdom, or its righteousness. Blessed Lord, let Your Spirit rise in great power and have dominion within us. May our hearts by Him be made the temple and the Kingdom in which You alone are glorified, in which Your glory fills all. Amen.

Chapter 16

SAVING THE WORLD FROM SIN

"If I depart I will send him (the Comforter) unto you. And when he is come, he will reprove the world of sin"—John 16:7,8.

The close connection between the two statements in these words of our Lord is not always noticed. Before the Holy Spirit was to reprove or convince the world of sin, He was first to come into the disciples. He was to dwell within them, and then, through them, He was to do His work of convicting the world of sin. "He shall testify of Me: And ye shall also bear witness" (John 15:26,27).

The disciples were to realize that the great work of the Holy Spirit, striving with man, convincing *the world* of sin, could only be done as He had a dwelling place *in them*. They were to be baptized with the Holy Spirit and with fire. They were to receive the power from on high with the one purpose of being the instruments through whom the Holy Spirit could reach the world.

The mighty, sin-convicting power of the Spirit

dwelling in them and working through them was the reason our blessed Lord sought to prepare them and us by these words. The lessons they teach us are very important.

The Spirit In Us

The Holy Spirit comes to us so that through us He may reach others. The Spirit is the Spirit of the Holy One, of the redeeming God. When He enters us, He does not change His nature or lose His divine character. He is still the Spirit of God striving with man and seeking his deliverance. Wherever He is not hindered by ignorance or selfishness, He makes the heart willing and bold to testify against sin. He does this as the Spirit of the crucified and exalted Christ.

For what purpose was it that *He* received the Spirit without measure? "The Spirit of the Lord God is upon Me; because (He) hath anointed Me to preach good tidings unto the meek; He hath sent Me. . .to proclaim liberty to the captives" (Isaiah 61:1). *It was this same Spirit of Jesus* whom He sent down on His Church. The Spirit would pursue His divine work in them as He had in Christ, as a light shining in, revealing and condemning, conquering the darkness, as "by the spirit of judgment, and by the spirit of burning" (Isaiah 4:4).

This is the power of divine conviction and conversion in the world. He would convince the world *as the Spirit dwelling in the Church*. "I will send Him *to you*, and when He is come, He

126

will reprove *the world."* It is in and through us that the Spirit can reach the world.

The Spirit can only reach others through us by first bringing us into perfect sympathy with Himself. He enters into us to become one with us. He becomes an attitude and a life within us. His work in us and through us becomes identical with our work.

The words of our Lord are frequently applied to believers in reference to the continued conviction of sin which He will have to do within them. This first work of the Spirit remains the basis of all His comforting and sanctifying work. It is only as He keeps alive the tender sense of the danger and shame of sinning again that we will be kept in our humble place before God—hiding in Jesus, our safety and strength.

As the Holy Spirit reveals and communicates the holy life of Christ within, the result will be a deeper sense of the sinfulness of sin. But the words mean more. If the Spirit through us is to convince the world of sin, He must first convince us of its sin. He must personally give us a sense of the guilt of the world's unbelief and rejection of our Savior. We must see each sin as the cause of that rejection and in some measure regard the sin as He does. Then there will be an inner unity between our witness and His witness against sin and for God. This will reach the conscience and carry conviction with a power that is from above.

A Humble Spirit

How easy it is in the power of the flesh to judge others without seeing the beam in our own eye. If we are indeed free from what we condemn, how easy it is to get a "holier than thou" attitude. We either testify and work in a wrong spirit and in our own strength, or we do not have the courage to work at all. We see the sin and the sinfulness of others, but not in a conviction that comes from the Holy Spirit.

When He convinces us of the sin of the world, His work bears two marks. One is the sacrifice of self, in the jealousy for God and His honor, combined with the deep and tender grief for the guilty. The other is a deep, strong faith in the possibility and power of deliverance.

We see each sin in the light of the cross. We see sin with its ugly guilt against God and its fearful power over the poor soul. We see sin condemned, atoned, put away, and conquered in Jesus. We learn to look upon the person as God looks upon him in His holiness. He hates sin with an infinite hatred, yet, He loves the person. He loves with such a love that He gives His Son, and the Son gives His life to destroy sin and set its captives free.

To obtain this conviction of sin, the believer needs to pray for it and to have his whole life under the leading of the Holy Spirit. The many different gifts of the Spirit all depend upon His personal indwelling and supremacy in the inner life. We must have the revelation in us that Christ gave His life to have sin destroyed.

When our Lord spoke the words, "He shall be in you," He opened up the secret of all the Spirit's teaching, sanctifying, and strengthening. The Spirit is the life of God. He enters in and becomes our life. As He sways and inspires the life, He will be able to work all He will in us.

Do you want to have this deep, spiritual conviction of the sin of the world so that you can be the person through whom the Spirit can convince sinners? Just yield your whole life and being to the Holy Spirit. Let the thought of the indwelling of the Holy God within you quiet your mind and heart into humble fear and worship. Surrender the great enemy that opposes Him—the flesh, the self-life—day by day to Him. Be content to aim at nothing less than being filled with the Spirit of Christ who gave Himself to die to take away sin.

As your life in the Spirit becomes healthy and strong, you will see more clearly and feel more keenly the sin around you. Your thoughts and feelings will be those of the Holy Spirit breathing in you. You will have a deep horror of sin and a deep faith in redemption from it. Your deep love for the souls who are living in sin, your willingness to die if men can be freed from it, will make you the fit instrument for the Spirit to convince the world of its sin.

The Spirit Brings Deliverance

The Spirit must dwell in us as the world's convincer of sin. "I will send Him *unto you,* and He will reprove (convince) *the world."* Offer yourself to Him to consider, feel, and bear the sins of those around you. Let the sins of the world be your concern as much as your own sin. Do they not dishonor God as much as yours? Are they not equally provided for in the great redemption? Does the Spirit dwelling in you long to convince them, too? The Holy Spirit dwelt in the body and nature of Jesus and was the source of what He felt, said, and did. Just as God worked out through Jesus the will of His holy love, so the Spirit now dwells in believers. They are His abode.

The one purpose for which there has been a Christ in the world, for which there is now a Holy Spirit, was that sin may be conquered and destroyed. This is the great purpose for which the baptism of the Spirit and of fire was given, that in and through believers He might convince of sin and deliver from it.

Put yourself into contact with the world's sin. Meet it in the love and faith of Jesus Christ, as the servant and helper of the needy and the wretched. Give yourself to prove the reality of your faith in Christ by your likeness to Him—thus will the Spirit convince the world of its unbelief.

Do not seek the full experience of the indwelling Spirit for your own selfish enjoyment. Seek Him so that He can do the Father's work through you as He did through Christ.

In unity of love with other believers work and pray that men may be saved out of sin. It is the life of believers in self-sacrificing love that will prove to the world that Christ is a reality and convince it of its sin of unbelief.

The comfort and success with which a man lives and carries on his business depends much upon his having a suitable building for it. When the Holy Spirit finds a believer whose heart is filled with God's thoughts of sin and God's power of redemption, He can do His work through that believer.

There is no surer way to receive a full measure of the Spirit than to be completely yielded to Him, to let the very mind of Christ regarding sin work in us. "He appeared to put away sin by the sacrifice of Himself" (Hebrews 9:26). What the Spirit was in Him, He seeks to be in us. What was true of Him, must in its measure be true of us.

Do you want to be filled with the Holy Spirit? Seek to have a clear impression of this—the Holy Spirit is in you to convince the world of sin. If you sympathize thoroughly with Him in this, if He sees that He can use you for this, He will dwell in you richly and work in you mightily. The one reason Christ came to die was to put away sin. The one work for which the Holy Spirit comes to men is to persuade them to give up sin. The one purpose for which the believer lives is to join in the battle against sin, to seek the will and the honor of his God. Let us be at one with Christ and His Spirit in their testimony against sin.

Evidence of the life and the Spirit of Christ will have its effect—the holiness, joy, love, and obedience to Christ will convince the world of its sin of unbelief. Christ's death was the entrance to His glory in the power of the Spirit.

In the same way our experience of the Spirit's indwelling will become fuller when our life is entirely given up to Him for His work of convincing the world of sin. The presence of Christ in us through the Spirit will carry its own conviction.

The great sin of the world is unbelief, the rejection of Christ. This is the very spirit of the world. This standpoint must decide my whole view of the world and my relationship to it. It is a world that by its very nature rejects Christ. This rejected Christ has left this world and gone to the Father. But He has left His people in it, and dwells in them by His Spirit, so that their holy life and their confession of Him may convince the world of its sin.

Complete surrender is needed if by my life He is to convince the world of the sin of unbelief. One thing is needed to do this. There must be intense, continued, united, believing prayer that the Father would strengthen us all with might by His Spirit.

Prayer

Lord Jesus make Your Church aware of the knowledge of her calling. May the world believe that the Father sent You and loves them as He loves You, His Son. Lord Jesus, lay the burden of the sin of the world on the hearts of Your people. May we live to be members of Your body in whom Your Spirit dwells and proves Your presence to the world. Take away everything that hinders You from manifesting Your presence and saving power in us. Lord Jesus, Your Spirit is come to us to convince the world. Let Him come and work in ever-growing power. Amen.

Chapter 17

EVANGELISM—YOU CAN PARTICIPATE

"Now there were in the church that was at Antioch certain prophets and teachers. . . .As they ministered to the Lord, and fasted, the Holy Ghost said, Separate me Barnabas and Saul for the work whereunto I have called them. And when they had fasted and prayed, and laid their hands on them, they sent them away. So they, being sent forth by the Holy Ghost departed unto Seleucia"—Acts 13:1-4.

It has been correctly said that the Acts of the Apostles might well have borne the name, the Acts of the Exalted Lord, or the Acts of the Holy Spirit. Christ gave this parting promise, "Ye shall receive power, after that the Holy Ghost is come upon you: and ye shall be *witnesses* unto Me. . .both in Jerusalem, and in all Judea, and in Samaria, and unto the uttermost parts of the earth" (Acts 1:8). This was one of those divine seed-words which contained the power of growth and the prophecy of its final perfection.

In the book of Acts we have the way traced in

which the promise received its fulfillment. It gives us the divine record of the coming and dwelling and working of the Holy Spirit as the power given to Christ's disciples to witness for Him before Jews and Gentiles.

The book of Acts reveals that the one aim and purpose of the descent of the Spirit was to reveal, in the disciples, the Lord's presence, guidance, and power. The Spirit equipped them to be His witnesses even to the uttermost parts of the earth. Sending missionaries to unbelievers is one purpose of the coming of the Spirit.

In the above passage from Acts 13, we have the first record of the Church being called to the work of missions. In the preaching of Philip at Samaria and Peter at Caesarea, we read of individual men exercising their function of ministry among those who were not of the Jews. In the preaching of the men of Cyprus and Cyrene to the Greeks at Antioch, we have men opening new paths where the leaders of the Church had not yet thought of going. But this guidance of the Spirit in separating special men was to become part of the organization of the Church. The whole community of believers was to share in the work for which the Spirit especially came to earth.

We cannot sufficiently praise God for the deepening interest in missions in our day. If this interest is to be permanent and fruitful in raising the work of the Church to the true level of Pentecostal power, we must learn the lesson of Antioch well. Mission work must find its initiative and its power in the distinct and direct acknowledgment of the guidance of the Holy Spirit.

Power For Missions

It has often been remarked that true mission work has always been born out of a revival in the Church. The Holy Spirit's quickening work stirs up new devotion to the blessed Lord whom He reveals, and to the lost to whom He belongs. It is in this state of mind that the voice of the Spirit is heard, urging the Lord's redeemed to work for Him.

It was this way at Antioch also. Certain prophets and teachers were spending part of their time ministering to the Lord and fasting. They served God through the church while maintaining the spirit of separation from the world.

Because their Lord was in heaven, they felt the need for close and continued communication in waiting for His orders. They understood that the Spirit could not have freedom to work unless they maintained direct fellowship with Him as their Master. For this reason they entered as much as possible into the fellowship of Christ's crucifixion of the flesh. "They ministered to the Lord and fasted."

Such were the men, such was their state of mind and their habit of life, when the Holy Spirit revealed to them that He had called two of their number to a special work. He called upon them to be His instruments in separating them, in the presence of the whole church, for that work.

The law of the Kingdom has not changed. It is still the Holy Spirit who has charge of all mission work. He will still reveal His will, in the appointment of work and selection of men, to those who are waiting on their Lord in service and separation. Once the Holy Spirit has taught men of faith and prayer to undertake His work, it is easy for others to admire and approve what they do. They see the harmony of their conduct with Scripture and seek to copy their example.

Yet, the real power of the Spirit's guiding and working may be present in only a small way. Supporters of mission work must still beg and plead for the interest from the Church. The command of the Lord is recorded in the Bible. However, the living voice of the Spirit, who reveals the Lord in living presence and power, is not heard.

It is not enough that Christians be stirred and urged to take a greater interest in the work, to pray and give more. There is a more urgent need. In the life of the individual, the indwelling of the Holy Spirit must become the distinguishing feature of the Christian life. In the fellowship of the Church, we must learn to wait more earnestly for the Holy Spirit's guidance in the selection of men and fields of labor. In the seeking of support, the Spirit's power must be expected to help the mission which has originated in much prayer and waiting on the Spirit.

However, dependence upon the Holy Spirit does not mean He has designed the work without us. There is much that needs to be done and cannot be done without our diligent labor. Information must be circulated. Readers must be found and kept. Funds must be raised. Prayer meetings must be kept up. Directors must meet, consult, and decide. All this must be done. But it will be done as a service pleasing to the Master, as long as it is done in the power of the Holy Spirit.

Oh, that the Church, and every member of it, might learn this lesson! The Spirit has come down from heaven to be the Spirit of missions, to inspire and empower Christ's disciples to witness for Him to the uttermost parts of the earth.

Successful Missionary Work

The origin, the progress, the success of missions are all His. It is the Spirit who awakens in the hearts of believers the jealousy for the Lord's honor, the compassion for souls, and the willing obedience to His commands. True missions find their source in these.

It is the Spirit who calls forth suitable men and women to go out. He opens the door and prepares the hearts of the heathen to desire to receive the Word. It is the Spirit who gives the increase. Even where Satan's seat is, He establishes the cross and gathers the redeemed of the Lord around it.

Missions are the special work of the Holy Spirit. No one may expect to be filled with the Spirit if he is not willing to be used for missions. No one who wishes to work or pray for missions needs to fear his weakness or poverty. The Holy Spirit is the power that can equip him to take his divinely-appointed place in the work of missions.

Let everyone who prays for missions and longs for more of a missionary spirit in the Church, pray first and most that in every believer personally, and in the Church, the power of the indwelling Spirit may have full control.

"And when they had fasted and prayed. . .*they sent them away*. So they, being *sent forth by the Holy Ghost* departed unto Seleucia." The sending forth was equally the work of the Church and of the Spirit. This is the normal relationship. There are men sent forth by the Holy Spirit alone. The Spirit does His work amid the opposition or indifference of the Church. There are also men sent forth by the Church alone. The Church thinks the work ought to be done and does it, but with little of the fasting and praying that recognizes the need for the Spirit. Blessed be the Church and blessed be the mission which the Spirit has originated.

Ten days' praying and waiting on earth and the Spirit's descent in fire—this was the birth of the Church at Jerusalem. After ministering, fasting, and praying, the Spirit sent forth Barnabas and Saul. This was the consecration of the Church to be a mission church at Antioch. The strength, the joy, the blessing of the Church and its missions comes from *waiting* for the power of the Spirit.

To any missionary who reads this in his far-off home, I say, "Be of good cheer, brother!" The Holy Spirit who is the mighty power of God is with you and in you. Depend on Him. Yield to Him. Wait for Him. The work is His. He will do it.

To every mission's director, supporter, contributor, intercessor, or helper in the great work of hastening the coming of the Kingdom, I say, "Brother! be of good cheer."

The secret of power lies in the baptism of the Holy Spirit. Let every Christian who would be a mission friend and mission worker desire to be filled with the Spirit. Let Christians who have experienced the baptism of the Spirit lift up a clear testimony to the Church and the world.

The Spirit still comes to us in power. He still moves and sends forth missionaries. He is still mighty to convict of sin and reveal Jesus, and to make thousands fall at His feet. He waits for us. Let us wait on Him. Let us welcome Him.

Prayer

My Father, I dedicate myself to You, to live and work, to pray and toil, to sacrifice and suffer for Your Kingdom. I accept by faith the wonderful gift of the Holy Spirit, the very Spirit of Christ, and yield myself to His indwelling. Give Your children the strength of the Holy Spirit so that Christ may possess our hearts and lives. May our desire be that the whole earth be filled with His glory. Amen.

Chapter 18

SET FREE!

"The law of the Spirit of life in Christ Jesus hath made me free from the law of sin and death. . . .if ye through the Spirit do mortify the deeds of the body, ye shall live"—Romans 8:2,13.

"But now we are delivered from the law, that being dead wherein we were held; that we should serve in newness of spirit, and not in the oldness of the letter"—Romans 7:6.

In the sixth chapter of Romans, Paul spoke of our having been made free from sin in Christ Jesus (verses 18 and 22). Our death to sin in Christ freed us from its dominion. We were made free from sin as a power, as a master. When we accepted Christ in faith, we became servants to righteousness and to God.

In the seventh chapter (verses 1-6) Paul spoke of our being made free from the law. "The strength of sin is the law" (1 Corinthians 15:56). Deliverance from sin and the law go together. Being made free from the law, we were united to the living Christ so that, in union with Him, we might now serve in newness of the Spirit (Romans 7:4-6). In these two passages (Romans 6 and 7:1-6), Paul presented being made free from sin and the law as a life to be accepted and maintained by faith.

According to the law of a gradual growth in the Christian life, the believer has to enter by faith into this union to walk in the power of the Spirit. As a matter of experience, almost all believers can testify that even after they have seen and accepted this teaching, their life is not what they hoped it would be. The descent into the experience of the second half of the seventh chapter of Romans is most real and painful.

However, there is no other way of learning the two great lessons the believer needs. One lesson is that the human will is powerless to work out divine righteousness in a person's life. The other lesson is the need for the conscious indwelling of the Holy Spirit as the only sufficient power for the life of a child of God.

The work of the indwelling Spirit is to glorify Christ and reveal Him within us. Corresponding to Christ's threefold office of prophet, priest, and king, we find that the work of the indwelling Spirit in the believer is set before us in three aspects: as enlightening, sanctifying, and strengthening. Christ speaks of this enlightening in His farewell words. He promises the Spirit of truth who will bear witness of Him and will take Christ's truth and declare it unto us.

In the epistles to the Romans and Galatians, the Spirit's sanctifying work is especially prominent. This was what was needed in churches whose members were brought out of idol worship. In the epistles to the Corinthians, the two aspects are combined. The Corinthian believers are taught that the Spirit can only enlighten as He sanctifies. (See 1 Corinthians 2, 3:1-3,16; 2 Corinthians 3.)

In the Acts of the Apostles, as we might expect, His strengthening for work is in the foreground. As the promised Spirit of power, He equips us to have a bold and blessed testimony in the midst of persecution and difficulty.

The Law And The Spirit

In the epistle to the church at Rome, the capital of the world, Paul was called of God to give a full and systematic account of His gospel and the plan of redemption. In Romans 1:17 he said, "the just shall live by faith." Paul paves the way to discuss that through faith both righteousness and life would come. In the first part of his argument (up to Romans 5:11), he teaches what the righteousness of faith is. He then proceeds (Romans 5:12-21) to prove how this righteousness is rooted in our living connection with the second Adam, and in a justification of life.

In the individual (Romans 6:1-13), this life comes through the believing acceptance of Christ's death to sin and His life to God as ours. It also comes from the willing surrender (Romans 6:14-23) to be servants of God and of righteousness. Paul proceeds to show that in Christ we are not only dead to sin, but to the law, too, as the strength of sin. The new law of the Spirit of life in Christ Jesus takes the place of the old.

Paul contrasted (Romans 6:13-23) the service of sin and of righteousness. He also contrasts the power and work of the Spirit with the service in the oldness of the letter (Romans 7:4).

In the following passage (Romans 7:14-25 and Romans 8:1-16), we have the contrast worked out. In the light of that contrast the two conditions can be understood. Each condition has its key-word, indicating the character of the life it describes. In the seventh chapter of Romans, we have the word *law* twenty times, and the word *Spirit* only once. On the contrary, in the eighth chapter of Romans, we find in its first sixteen verses the word *Spirit* sixteen times. The contrast is between the Christian life in the law and the Spirit.

Paul very boldly said we are dead to sin and made free from sin that we might become servants to righteousness and to God (Romans, chapter 6). He also said we were made dead to the law, so that "being dead wherein we were held; that we should serve in newness of spirit, and not in the oldness of the letter." We have here, then, a double advance on the teaching of the sixth chapter of Romans. There it was death to sin and freedom from it, here it is death to the law and freedom from it. There it was "newness of life" (Romans 6:4) as an objective reality secured to us in Christ. Here it is "newness of spirit" (Romans

7:6) as a subjective experience made ours by the indwelling of the Spirit. The believer who wants to know and enjoy the life in the Spirit must know what life in the law is and how completely free he is made by the Spirit.

Freedom From Sin And The Law

In the account of the Christian life in the epistle of Romans, there is a distinct advance from step to step. The eighth chapter teaches us that when the Spirit empowers our life and walk, we can fully possess and enjoy the riches of grace that are ours in Christ.

The second verse of the eighth chapter is the key verse. It reveals the wonderful secret of how our freedom from sin and the law may become a living and abiding experience. A believer may know that he is free and yet have to mourn that his experience is that of a wretched captive. The freedom is entirely *in* Christ Jesus, and the maintenance of the living union with Him is distinctly and entirely a work of divine power. The divine Spirit dwells within us to help us yield to His working. Then, we can stand perfect and complete in the freedom with which Christ makes us free.

Believers In Bondage

In the description Paul gives of the life of a believer, who is still held in bondage to the law and seeks to fulfill it, there are three expressions in which the characteristics of that condition are summed up. The first is the word *flesh*. "I am carnal (fleshly), sold under sin. . . .in me (that is, in my flesh) dwelleth no good thing" (Romans 7:14,18).

If we want to understand the word carnal, we must refer to Paul's exposition of it in 1 Corinthians 1-3. He uses it there of Christians who, though regenerate, have not yielded themselves entirely to the Spirit so as to become spiritual. They have the Spirit, but allow the flesh to prevail. As long as they have the Spirit, but do not fully accept His deliverance and strive in their own strength, they do not and cannot become spiritual. Paul here describes the regenerate man. He lives by the Spirit, but, according to Galatians 5:25, does not walk by the Spirit. He has the new spirit within him, according to Ezekial 36:26, but he has not intelligently and practically accepted God's own Spirit to dwell and rule within that spirit as the life of his life. He is still carnal.

The second expression we find in Romans 7:18: "To will is present with me; but how to perform that which is good I find not." In Romans 7:15-21, Paul attempts to make clear the painful state of powerlessness in which the law, and the effort to fulfill it, leaves a person. "For the good that I would I do not: but the evil which I would not, that I do" (verse 19). *Willing, but not doing*— such is the service of God in the oldness of the letter, in the life before Pentecost. "Watch and pray, that ye enter not into temptation: the spirit indeed is willing, but the flesh is weak" (Matthew 26:41). The renewed spirit of the man has accepted and consented to the will of God. But the secret of the indwelling power is not yet known.

In those, on the contrary, who know what the life in the Spirit is, God works both to will *and to do*. The Christian testifies, "I can do all things through Christ which strengtheneth me" (Philippians 4:13). But this is only possible through faith and the Holy Spirit. As long as the believer has not consciously been made free from the law, continual failure will attend his efforts to do the will of God. He may even delight in the law of God after the inward man, but the power is lacking. It is only when he submits to the law of faith that he may be joined to the living Jesus, working in him through His Holy Spirit. Then he will indeed bring forth fruit unto God. "Wherefore, my brethren, ye also are become dead to the law by the body of Christ; that ye should be married to another, even to Him who is raised from the dead, that we should bring forth fruit unto God" (Romans 7:4).

The third expression we must note is in Romans 7:23: "I see another law in my members. . .bringing me into captivity to the law of sin which is in my members." This word, *captivity,* suggests the idea of slaves sold into bondage without the liberty or the power to do as they will. They point back to what Paul had said in the beginning of the chapter, that we have been *made free* from the law. Here is evidently one who does not yet know that liberty.

This leads us to what Paul is to say in Romans 8:2: "The law of the Spirit of life in Christ Jesus

hath made me free from the law of sin and death.''
Paul here contrasts the two opposing laws: the one
of sin and death in the members, the other of the
Spirit of life ruling and quickening even the mor-
tal body. Under the former we have seen the
believer sighing as a wretched captive. In the second half of the sixth chapter of Romans, Paul
addressed the believer as made free from sin. By
voluntary surrender he has become a servant to
God and to righteousness. He has forsaken the service of sin, and yet it often masters him.

The promise that sin will not have control over
us has not been realized for many Christians. The
desire is present, but the knowledge of how to do
it is lacking. ''O wretched man that I am! who
shall deliver me from the body of this death?''
(Romans 7:24). This is the cry of helplessness
amid all his efforts to keep the law. ''I thank God,
through Christ Jesus our Lord'' (Romans 7:28).
This is the answer of faith that claims deliverance
in Christ from this power that has held him captive. That deliverance is a new law, a mightier
force, an actual power making us free from sin.

Life In Christ

From the very first beginnings of the new life, it
was the Spirit who taught us faith in Christ. On
our first entering into justification, it was He who
shed abroad the love of God in our hearts. It was
He who led us to see Christ as our life as well as
our righteousness. But all this was in most cases
still accompanied with much ignorance of His

presence and of the great need for His almighty power.

The freedom with which we have been made free in Christ cannot be fully accepted or experienced as long as there is a legal spirit. It is only by the Spirit of Christ within us that the full liberation takes place. As in the oldness of the letter, so in the newness of the Spirit, a twofold relationship exists. There is the law over me and outside of me, and there is the law of sin in my members deriving its strength. In being made free from the law, there is the liberty in Christ offered to my faith. There is also the personal possession of that liberty to be had solely through the Spirit dwelling and ruling in my members, even as the law of sin had done. This alone can change the captive into the ransomed.

Liberty In The Spirit

How are we to regard the two states set before us in Romans 7:14-23 and Romans 8:1-16? Are they interchangeable or successive or simultaneous? Many people have thought these changes are a description of the varying experience of the believer's life. When the believer is able to do what is good and to live pleasing to God, he experiences the grace of chapter 8. However, the consciousness of sin or shortcoming plunges him again into the wretchedness of chapter 7. Although now the one and then the other experiences may be more pronounced, each day brings the experience of both.

Other people have felt that this is not the life of a believer as God would have it or as the provision of God's grace has placed it within our reach. They saw that a life in the freedom with which Christ makes free, when the Holy Spirit dwells within us, is within our reach. As they entered upon this life, it was as if they had left the experience of Romans 7 behind forever, and they cannot but look upon it as Israel's wilderness life—a life never more to be returned to. There are many who can testify that light came to them when they saw the blessed transition from the bondage of the law to the liberty of the Spirit.

No matter how much we understand this, it does not fully satisfy. The believer feels that there is not a day that he gets beyond the words, "in me (that is, in my flesh) dwelleth no good thing" (Romans 7:18). Even when kept most joyously in the will of God and strengthened not only to will but also to do, he knows that it is not he, but the grace of God. And so the believer comes to see that, not the two experiences, but the two states are simultaneous. Even when his experience is most fully that of the law of the Spirit of life in Christ Jesus making him free, he still bears about with him the body of sin and death.

The deliverance from the power of sin and the song of thanks to God are the continuous experience of the power of the life maintained by the Spirit of Christ. As I am led of the Spirit, I am not under the law. Its spirit of bondage, its weakness through the flesh, and the sense of condemnation it brings are cast out by the liberty of the Spirit.

The believer who wants to live fully in this freedom of the life in Christ Jesus will easily understand the path in which he must learn to walk. The eighth chapter of Romans is the goal to which the sixth and seventh chapters lead. In faith the believer will first have to study and accept all that is taught in these two earlier chapters of his being in Christ Jesus—dead to sin and alive to God, free from sin and the law, and married to Christ.

"If ye continue in My word. . . .ye shall know the truth, and the truth shall make you free" (John 8:31,32). Let the Word of God, as it teaches you your union with Christ, be the life-soil in which your faith and life has its roots. Abide and dwell in it, and let it abide in you. The way to rise and reach each higher truth of Scripture is to meditate, to hold fast, to hide in the heart the word of this gospel, and to assimilate it in faith and patience.

The passage through the experience of carnality and captivity of the law may appear to be anything but progress. However, it is in the utter despair of self that entire surrender to the Spirit is strengthened to keep us in the freedom with which Christ makes us free. The way of entrance into the liberty of the Spirit is to cease from all hope in the flesh and the law.

To walk in the paths of this new life, it will be helpful to remember what is meant by the expression the Word so distinctly uses, a "walk after the Spirit" (Romans 8:1). The Spirit is to lead, to decide, and to show the path. This implies surrender, obedience, a waiting to be guided. He is to be the ruling power. We are in all things to live and act under the law, the legislation, the dominion of the Spirit. We must have a holy fear to grieve Him, a tender watchfulness to know His leading, an habitual faith in His hidden but sure presence.

The words which Paul uses toward the close of this section are to express our one aim: "If ye, through the Spirit, do mortify (make to die) the deeds of the body, ye shall live" (Romans 8:13). The fulfillment of this verse is seen in the Holy Spirit's possessing and inspiring all the powers of our spirit and soul. This is the "salvation through sanctification of the Spirit" (2 Thessalonians 2:13) to which we have been chosen.

Walk In The Spirit

The visible manifestation of Christ to us and His work is much more understandable than the revelation of the Spirit within us. In seeking the leading of the Spirit, faith is called for. The Spirit hides Himself away in union with our weakness. It requires patient perseverance in believing and obeying to come into the full consciousness of His having indeed undertaken to do all our living for us. Walking after the Spirit requires a fresh anointing day by day from the Holy One, in fellowship with Christ and in waiting on the Father. Here, if ever, the word is needed, "Only believe!"

Believe in the Father and His promise! Believe in the Son and His life: "Your life is hid with Christ in God" (Colossians 3:3). Believe in the Spirit, as the bearer, communicator, and maintainer of the life and presence of Jesus! Believe in Him as already being within you! Believe in His power and faithfulness to work in you in a way that is divine and beyond your conception. Believe, "the law of the Spirit of life in Christ Jesus hath made me free from the law of sin and death."

Prayer

Beloved Lord Jesus, I humbly ask You to make clear to us the blessed secret of the life of the Spirit. Teach us what it means to become dead to the law, so that our service of God is no longer in the oldness of the letter. Blessed Master, teach me to serve You in the newness and the liberty of the Spirit of life. Teach me to yield myself in large and wholehearted faith to the Holy Spirit, so that my life may be lived in the glorious liberty of the children of God. Amen.

Chapter 19

HOW TO BE A CHILD OF GOD

"For as many as are led by the Spirit of God, they are the sons of God"—Romans 8:14.

Many Christians think the leading of the Spirit is just the suggestion of thoughts in their mind for our guidance. In their daily lives, they would like to have some indication from the Spirit of the right choice when making a decision or when in need of direction. However, they long and ask for such guidance in vain. When they think they have attained it, there is no assurance, comfort, or success which they thought should be the seal from the Spirit. And so the precious truth of the Spirit's leading, instead of being a source of comfort and of strength, becomes cause for perplexity.

The error in this matter comes from not accepting that the teaching and the leading of the Spirit are first given in the life, not in the mind. The life is stirred and strengthened. The life becomes the light. As conformity to the world is crucified and dies, as we deliberately deny the will of the flesh, we *are renewed in the spirit* of our mind. In this way the mind becomes able to *prove and know* the good and perfect and acceptable will of God (Romans 12:2).

This connection between the practical sanctifying work of the Spirit in our inner life, and His leading, comes out very clearly in Scripture. "If ye through the Spirit, do mortify the deeds of the body, ye shall live," we read in Romans 8:13. Then follows immediately, "For as many as are led by the Spirit of God, they are the sons of God" (verse 14). As many as allow themselves to be led by Him in this denying of the flesh, these are the sons of God.

The Holy Spirit is the Spirit of the holy life which there was and is in Christ Jesus, and which works in us as a divine life-power. He is the Spirit of holiness, and only as such will He lead us. God works in us both to will and to do His good pleasure through Him. God made us perfect in every good work to do His will through the Spirit's working in us that which is pleasing in His sight. To be led of the Spirit implies the surrender to His work as He convicts of sin and cleanses soul and body for His temple. It is the indwelling Spirit, filling, sanctifying, and ruling the heart and life, that He enlightens and leads.

The Spirit Inspires

Only the spiritual mind can discern spiritual things and can receive the leadings of the Spirit. The mind must grow spiritually to become capable of spiritual guidance. Paul told the Corinthians that, although born again, they were still carnal. They were babes in Christ, and he had not been able to teach them spiritual truth. If this holds true of the teaching that comes through man, how much more we need that direct teaching of the Spirit by which He leads into all truth!

The deepest mysteries of Scripture, as far as they are understood by human thought, can be studied and even taught by the unsanctified mind. But I cannot repeat it too often that the leading of the Spirit does not begin in the region of thought or feeling. The Holy Spirit makes His home deeper down in the life itself. In this hidden laboratory of the inner life is the power that molds the will and fashions the character in our spirit. There He breathes and moves and guides. He leads by inspiring us with a life and attitude out of which right purposes and decisions come forth.

Prayer teaches us that it is only to spiritual understanding that the knowledge of God's will can be given. Spiritual understanding only comes with the growth of the spiritual man and the faithfulness to the spiritual life. The believer who wants the leading of the Spirit must yield himself to have his life completely possessed and filled with the Spirit.

After Christ had been baptized with the Spirit, the Scripture says, "being full of the Holy Ghost. . .(He) was led by the Spirit into the wilderness" (Luke 4:1). "Jesus returned in the power of the Spirit into Galilee" (Luke 4:14). He began His ministry in Nazareth with the words, "The

Spirit of the Lord is upon Me" (Luke 4:18).

In order to enjoy the leading of the Spirit, we need a very teachable mind. The Spirit is not only hindered by the flesh as the power that commits sin, but still more by the flesh that seeks to serve God. To be able to discern the Spirit's teaching, the ear must be closed to all that the flesh and its wisdom has to say.

In all our worship of God, our study of His Word, and our work for Him, there must be a continued distrust and denial of self. There must be a very definite waiting on God by the Holy Spirit to teach and lead us. The believer who daily and hourly waits for divine leading, for the light of knowledge and of duty, will assuredly receive it. If you want to be led of the Spirit, give up your will and wisdom as well as your whole life and being. The fire will descend and consume the sacrifice.

Led By Faith

The leading of the Spirit must especially be a thing of faith in two ways. The beginning of the leading will come when we learn to cultivate and act upon the statement: The Holy Spirit is in me, and is doing His work. The Spirit's indwelling is the crowning piece of God's work of redemption. Here, if anywhere, faith is needed. Faith is the faculty of the soul which recognizes the unseen, the divine. It receives the impression of the divine presence when God draws near. It accepts what the Holy Spirit brings and gives to us.

The Holy Spirit is the most intimate communication of the divine life. Here faith may not judge by what it feels or understands, but simply submits to God to let Him do what He has said. It meditates and worships. Faith prays and trusts. It yields the whole soul in adoring acceptance and thanksgiving to the Savior's word, "He shall be in you" (John 14:17). It rejoices in the assurance: The Holy Spirit, the mighty power of God, dwells within. I may depend upon it—He will lead me.

Along with this more general faith in the indwelling of the Spirit, faith also has to be exercised in regard to each part of the leading. When there is a question I have laid before the Lord, and my soul has waited for His leading, I must in faith trust God that His guidance is not withheld. As we have said before, we must not expect the ordinary leading of the Spirit in sudden impulses or strong impressions or heavenly voices. The time may come when our very thoughts and feelings are the conscious vehicles of His blessed voice. But we must leave this to Him and the growth of our spiritual capacity. The lower steps of the ladder are let down low enough for the weakest to reach.

God wants every child of His to be led by the Spirit every day. Begin the path of following the Spirit's leading by believing, not only that the Spirit is within you, but that He does at once undertake the work for which you ask and trust Him. Yield yourself to God in undivided surrender. Believe with implicit confidence that God's acceptance of the surrender means that the Spirit is in charge of you. Through Him Jesus guides and rules and saves you.

Are we in danger of being led away by the imaginings of our own hearts? Could we consider as leading of the Spirit something that proves to be a delusion of the flesh? And if so, where is our safeguard against such error? The answer ordinarily given to this last question is: The Word of God. And yet that answer is half the truth. The answer is: The Word of God as taught by the Spirit of God. Let us on the one hand remember that, as all the Word of God is given by the Spirit of God, each word must be interpreted to us by that same Spirit. We do not have to repeat that this interpretation comes alone from the indwelling Spirit.

It is only the spiritual man, whose inner life is under the dominion of the Spirit, who can discern the spiritual meaning of the Word. All the Word is given by the Spirit, so His great work is to honor that Word and to unfold the fullness of divine truth treasured there. Our assurance of safety in the path of the Spirit's guidance is in the Word and Spirit both dwelling richly within us and yielded to in implicit obedience.

Dead To Sin

This brings us back to the lesson we urged at the beginning: The leading of the Spirit is inseparable from the sanctifying of the Spirit. Let each one who would be led of the Spirit begin by giving himself to be led of the Word as far as he knows it. Begin at the beginning. Obey the commandments. Give up every sin. Give everything up to the voice of conscience. Give up everything to God and let Him have His way. As a son of God place yourself at the entire disposal of the Spirit, to follow where He leads. And the Spirit Himself will bear witness with your spirit that you are indeed a child of God enjoying all a child's privileges in his Father's love and guidance.

Prayer

Father, I yield myself to You as Your child, in everything to be led by Your Spirit. I forsake my own wisdom, my own will, my own way. Daily I wait in deep dependence on a guidance from above. May my spirit be hushed in silence before Your Holy Spirit, while I wait to let Him rule within. As I, through the Spirit, make dead the deeds of the body, may I be transformed by the renewing of my mind to know Your good and perfect will. May my whole being be so under the rule of the indwelling, sanctifying Spirit, that the spiritual understanding of Your will may indeed be the rule of my life. Amen.

Chapter 20

REVITALIZING YOUR PRAYER LIFE

"Likewise the Spirit also helpeth our infirmities: for we know not what we should pray for as we ought: but the Spirit itself maketh intercession for us with groanings which cannot be uttered. And he that searcheth the hearts knoweth what is the mind of the Spirit, because he maketh intercession for the saints according to the will of God"—Romans 8:26,27.

The ministry of the Holy Spirit that leads us most deeply into the understanding of the mystery of the Holy Trinity is the work He does as the Spirit of prayer. We have the Father to whom we pray and who hears prayer. We have the Son through whom we pray and through whom we receive and appropriate the answer. And we have the Holy Spirit, who prays in us according to the will of God with unutterable sighings.

How wonderful and real is the divine work of God on the throne, who graciously hears and effectually answers prayer. How divine is the work of the Son who intercedes and secures and transmits the answer from above. How wonderful is the work of the Holy Spirit in us in the prayer which waits and obtains the answer. The intercession within is as divine as the intercession above. Let us try to understand why this should be so and what it teaches us.

In the creation of the world, it was the work of the Spirit to put Himself into contact with the dark and lifeless matter of chaos, and by His quickening energy to give it the power of life and fruitfulness. It was only after it had been vitalized by Him that the Word of God gave it form and called forth all the different types of life and beauty we now see. In the creation of man, it was also the Spirit that was breathed into the body that had been formed from the ground. The Spirit united itself with what would otherwise be dead matter.

In the person of Jesus, a body was prepared for Him by the Spirit. Through the Spirit, His body was quickened from the grave. It is also through the Spirit that our bodies are the temples of God. The very members of our body are made the members of Christ. We think of the Spirit in connection with the spiritual nature of God, far removed from the weakness of matter. It is the work of the Spirit to unite Himself with what is material and lift it up into His own Spirit-nature. He then develops what will be the highest type of perfection—a spiritual body.

This view of the Spirit's work is essential to the understanding of the place He takes in the divine work of redemption. In each part of that work there is a special place assigned to each of the Three Persons of the Holy Trinity. In the Father we have the unseen God, the author of all. In the Son of God revealed, made manifest, and brought near we have the form of God. In the Spirit of God, we have the power of God dwelling in the human body and working in us what the Father and the Son have for us. This is true not only in the individual, but in the Church as a whole. What the Father has purposed, and the Son has procured, can be appropriated in the Body of Christ only through the active operation of the Holy Spirit.

Praying In The Spirit

In the life of faith and prayer there are operations of the Spirit in which the Word of God is made clear to our understanding, and our faith knows to express what it needs and asks. But there are also operations of the Spirit where He works desires and yearnings in our spirit which only God can discover and understand. The real thirst is for God Himself, and the real longing is to know the love that passes all knowledge. When these aspirations take possession of us, we begin to pray for what cannot be expressed, and our only comfort is that the Spirit prays with His inutterable yearnings in a region and a language which God alone knows and understands.

To the Corinthians Paul says, "I will pray with the spirit, and I will pray with the understanding also" (1 Corinthians 14:15). To pray with the understanding is easy and universal. We need to be reminded that there must also be the prayer with the Spirit—the "praying in the Holy Spirit" (Jude verse 20; Ephesians 6:18).

We need to give each of the twofold operations of the Spirit its place. God's Word must dwell in us richly. Our faith must seek to hold it clearly and intelligently and to plead it in prayer. To have the words of Christ abiding in us, filling life and conduct, is one of the secrets of acceptable prayer. And yet we must always remember that in the inner sanctuary of our being, in the region of the unutterable and inconceivable (1 Corinthians 2:6), the Spirit prays for us things we do not know and cannot express.

As we grow in the understanding of the Holy Spirit who dwells within, we will recognize how infinitely beyond the conception of our mind must be that divine hunger with which He draws heavenward. We will feel the need to cultivate the activity of faith which seeks to grasp and obey God's Word and from that to learn to pray. Let us believe that where heart and flesh fail, God is the strength of our heart. His Holy Spirit within us in the innermost sanctuary of our spirit, within the veil, does His unceasing work of intercession and prays according to God within us. As we pray, let us worship in holy stillness and yield ourselves to that blessed Paraclete who truly is the Spirit of supplication.

Praying For The Church

"Because He maketh intercession for the

saints." Why does the apostle not say *for us*? Instead, he uses the expression, *the saints*. Paul thinks of the Church throughout the world. It is the special work of the Spirit, as dwelling in every member, to make the Body of Christ realize its unity. As selfishness disappears and the believer becomes more spiritually minded, he feels himself more identified with the Body as a whole. He sees how the health and prosperity of the Church will be his own. He learns what it is to "(Pray) always with all prayer and supplication in the Spirit, and watching thereunto with all perseverance. . .for all saints" (Ephesians 6:18).

When we give ourselves to the work of praying for all the Church, the Spirit will have the freedom to do His work of intercession. In intercessory prayer, we may count upon the deep, unutterable, but all-prevailing intercession of the Spirit.

What a privilege to be the temple out of which the Holy Spirit cries to the Father His unceasing "Abba!" and offers His unutterable intercession too deep for words. The eternal Son dwelt in the flesh in Jesus of Nazareth and prayed to the Father as man. In the same way, the eternal Spirit will dwell in us, sinful flesh, to train us to speak with the Father even as the Son did. We need only to yield ourselves to this blessed Spirit to share in that intercessory work through which the Kingdom of God can only be revealed.

The Lord, on His last night, gave us those wonderful prayer promises with the phrase, *"Ask what ye will."* He meant for us to have the Holy

Spirit praying in us, guiding our desires, and strengthening our faith. He expected us to give our whole being to the indwelling of the Spirit, that He might have freedom to pray in us according to God.

"We know not what we should pray for as we ought." How often this has been a burden and a sorrow! Let it from now on be a comfort. When we do not know, we may stand aside and give place to One who does know. We may believe that in our stammering utterances the mighty intercessor is pleading. Let us not be afraid to believe that within our ignorance and feebleness the Holy Spirit is hidden, doing His work.

Prayer

Father, show me all that hinders the Spirit from taking full possession of me and filling me with the consciousness of His presence. Let my innermost being and my outer life all be under His leading. May I have the spiritual understanding that knows to ask according to Your will and the living faith that receives what it asks. And when I do not know what or how to pray, teach me to bow in silent worship and keep waiting before You, knowing that the Spirit breathes the wordless prayer which You alone can understand. Blessed God, I am a temple of the Holy Spirit. I yield myself for Him to use me as the Spirit of intercession. May my whole heart be so filled with the longing for Christ's honor and His love for the lost

that my life may become one unutterable cry for
the coming of Your Kingdom. Amen.

Chapter 21

THE HOLY SPIRIT AND
YOUR CONSCIENCE

"I say the truth in Christ, I lie not, my conscience also bearing me witness in the Holy Ghost"—Romans 9:1.

"The Spirit itself beareth witness with our spirit"—Romans 8:16.

God's highest glory is *His holiness*. He hates and destroys the evil and loves and works the good. In man, conscience has the same work. It condemns sin and approves the right. Conscience is the remains of God's image in man, the nearest approach to the divine in him. It is the guardian of God's honor amid the ruin of the fall. As a consequence, God's work of redemption must always begin with conscience. The Spirit of God is the Spirit of His holiness. Conscience is a spark of the divine holiness. Harmony between the work of the Holy Spirit and the work of conscience is most essential.

The believer who wants to be filled with the Holy Spirit must first yield to conscience the place of honor which belongs to it. Faithfulness to conscience is the first step in the path of restoration to the Holiness of God. It is the work of conscience to witness to our having a right sense of duty and a right relationship with God. It is the work of the Spirit to witness to God's acceptance of our faith in Christ and our obedience to Him. As the Christian life progresses, the Spirit and conscience will say with Paul, in regard to all our conduct: "My conscience also bearing me witness in the Holy Ghost."

Conscience can be compared to the window of a room, through which the light of heaven shines into it and through which we can look out and see all that heaven shines on. The heart is the chamber in which our life dwells—our soul with its abilities and affections. On the walls of that chamber, the law of God is written. Even in unbelievers it is still partly legible, though sadly darkened and defaced. In the believer the law is written anew by the Holy Spirit, in letters of light. They are often dim at first, but grow clearer and glow brighter as they are freely exposed to the action of the light without.

The light that shines in makes every sin I commit manifest and condemns it. If the sin is not confessed and forsaken, the stain remains. Conscience becomes defiled because the mind refused the teaching of the light. (See Titus 1:15.) And so with one sin after another, the window gets darker and darker, until the light can hardly shine through at all. Then the Christian can continue sinning undisturbed, with his conscience to a large extent blinded and without feeling.

In His work of renewal, the Holy Spirit does not create new faculties. Instead, He renews and sanctifies those already existing. Conscience is the work of the Spirit of God the creator. As the redeeming Spirit of God, His first concern is to restore what sin has defiled. By restoring our conscience to healthy action and revealing in it the wonderful grace of Christ, He enables the believer to live a life in the full light of God's favor. We can walk in the light as long as the window of our heart that looks heavenward is cleansed and kept clean.

Light On The Conscious

The work of the Spirit on conscience is a three-fold one. Through conscience the Spirit causes *the light of God's holy law* to shine into the heart. A room may have its curtains drawn and even its shutters closed. This cannot prevent the lightning flash from time to time shining into the darkness. Conscience may be sin-stained and seared so that the strong man within dwells in perfect peace. When the lightning from Sinai flashes into the heart, conscience wakes up, and it is at once ready to admit the condemnation. Both the law and the gospel, with their call to repentance and their conviction of sin, appeal to conscience. Yet, it is not until conscience has said *amen* to the charge of transgression and unbelief that deliverance can truly come.

It is through conscience that the Spirit likewise causes *the light of mercy* to shine. When the windows of a house are stained, they need to be washed. "How much more shall the blood of Christ. . .purge (cleanse) your conscience" (Hebrews 9:14). The whole aim of the precious blood of Christ is to reach the conscience, to silence its accusations, and to cleanse it until it testifies that every stain is removed: "(a heart) sprinkled from an evil testimony, "For our rejoicing is this, the testimony of our conscience, that in simplicity (holiness) and godly sincerity. . .by the grace of God, we have had our conversation (behavior) in the world" (2 Corinthians 1:12). (See also Acts 23:1; 24:16; 2 Timothy 1:3.)

Let us note these words well: "For our rejoicing is this, the testimony of our conscience." When the window is kept clean and bright by our abiding in the light, we can have fellowship with the Father and the Son. "Beloved, if our heart condemns us not, then have we confidence toward God. . .because we keep His commandments, and do those things that are pleasing in His sight" (1 John 3:21,22).

Maintaining A Clean Conscience

The daily maintenance of a good conscience toward God is essential to the life of faith. The believer must aim at, must be satisfied with, nothing less than this. He may be assured that it is within his reach.

The believers in the Old Testament, by faith,

had the witness that they pleased God (Hebrews 11:4,5,6,39). In the New Testament it is presented to us, not only as a command to be obeyed, but as a grace to be brought about by God Himself. "That ye might walk worthy of the Lord *unto all pleasing. . .strengthened with all might,* according to His glorious power" (Colossians 1:10,11).

The more we seek this testimony of conscience that we are doing what is pleasing to God, the more we will feel the freedom to look at once to the blood that cleanses. Then our assurance will be stronger knowing that the indwelling sinfulness is covered by that blood as well. "If we walk in the light, as He is in the light, we have fellowship one with another, and the blood of Jesus Christ His Son cleanseth us from all sin" (1 John 1:7).

Often, faith is weak because we lack a clean conscience. Notice how closely Paul connects them in 1 Timothy: "(Love) out of a pure heart, and of a good conscience, and of faith unfeigned" (verse 1:5); "holding faith, and a good conscience; which some having put away concerning faith have made shipwreck" (verse 19). Look especially at 1 Timothy 3:9, "Holding the mystery of the faith in a pure conscience."

The conscience is the seat of faith. The believer who wants to grow strong in faith and have boldness with God must know that he is pleasing Him. (See 1 John 3:21,22.) Jesus said most distinctly that it is for those who love Him and keep His commandments that the promise of the Spirit is meant. How can we confidently claim these promises, unless in childlike simplicity our conscience can testify that we fulfill the conditions?

Before the Church can rise to the height of her holy calling as intercessor and claim these unlimited promises as within her reach, believers will have to draw near to their Father. They must glory, like Paul, in the testimony of their conscience, that by the grace of God they are walking in holiness and godly sincerity. We must give up man's ideas of attaining and accept God's promises as the only standard of what we are to be.

Dealing With Sin

How is this blessed life to be attained in which we daily appeal to God and men? "I say the truth in Christ, my conscience also bearing me witness in the Holy Ghost." First, we must bow very low under the reproofs of conscience. Do not be content with the general confession that there is a great deal wrong. Beware of confusing actual sinning with the involuntary workings of the sinful nature. If the latter are to be conquered and made dead by the indwelling Spirit (Romans 8:13), you must first deal with the former.

Begin with some single sin and give your conscience time in silent submission and humiliation to reprove you. Say to your Father that in this one thing you are, by His grace, going to obey. Accept anew Christ's wonderful offer to take entire possession of your heart to dwell in you as Lord and keeper. Trust Him by His Holy Spirit to do this, even when you feel weak and helpless. Remember that obedience is the only way to prove the reality of your surrender to Him or your interest in His work and grace. And vow in faith that by God's grace you will exercise yourself "to have always a conscience void of offense toward God, and toward man" (Acts 24:16).

When you have begun this practice with one sin, proceed with others, step by step. As you are faithful in keeping your conscience pure, the light will shine more brightly from heaven into your heart, discovering sin you had not noticed before. God's light will bring out distinctly the law written by the Spirit you had not been able to read. Be willing to be taught. Be trustfully sure that the Spirit will teach. Every honest effort to keep your conscience clean in the light of God will be met with the aid of the Spirit. Only yield yourself heartily and entirely to God's will and to the power of His Holy Spirit.

As you listen to the reproofs of conscience and give yourself completely to do God's will, your courage will grow so strong that it is possible to have a conscience void of offense. The witness of conscience, as to what you are doing and will do by grace, will be met by the witness of the Spirit as to what Christ is doing and will do. In childlike simplicity, you will seek to begin each day with the simple prayer: "Father! there is nothing between You and I. My conscience has been cleansed in the blood and bears me witness. In everything I would do Your will. Your Spirit dwells in me and leads me and makes me strong in Christ.''

In a well-ordered house, the windows are kept clean, especially where the owner loves to rest and look out on some beautiful scene. See to it every day that the windows of your heart are kept clean. Do not allow the shadow of a cloud to obscure the light from above shining on you or your look of love as it seeks the Father's face above. Involuntary sin is at once cleansed by the blood of Jesus if faith claims it. Let every failure be at once confessed and cleansed, also. Be content with nothing less than walking in the light of His countenance all day long.

Prayer

O my Father, I desire this day to walk before You with a good conscience, to do nothing that might grieve You or my blessed Lord Jesus. May the cleansing in the blood be a living, continual, and most effective deliverance from the power of sin, binding and strengthening me to serve You. May my whole walk with You be in the joy of the united witness of conscience and Spirit that I am pleasing to You. Amen.

Chapter 22

HOW TO ACQUIRE WISDOM

"My preaching was not with enticing words of man's wisdom, but in demonstration of the Spirit and of power: That your faith should not stand in the wisdom of men, but in the power of God. Howbeit we speak wisdom among them that are perfect: yet not the wisdom of this world. . .but we speak the wisdom of God in a mystery, even the hidden wisdom. . .which none of the princes of this world knew. . . .But God hath revealed them unto us by his Spirit. . . .Now we have received, not the spirit of the world, but the Spirit which is of God; that we might know the things that are freely given to us of God. Which things also we speak, not in the words which man's wisdom teacheth, but which the Holy Ghost teacheth. . . .But the natural man receiveth not the things of the Spirit of God. . .But he that is spiritual judgeth all things"—1 Corinthians 2:4-15.

In this passage Paul contrasts the spirit of the world and the Spirit of God. The point in which the contrast especially comes out is in the wisdom or knowledge of the truth. It was in seeking knowledge that man fell. It was in the pride of knowledge that heathenism had its origin: "Professing themselves to be wise, they became fools" (Romans 1:22).

It was in wisdom, philosophy, and the search after truth that the Greeks sought their glory. It was in the knowledge of God's will, "the form of the knowledge and of the truth in the law" (Romans 2:20), that the Jew made his boast. And yet when Christ, the wisdom of God, appeared on earth, Jew and Greek combined to reject Him.

Man's wisdom, whether in possession of a revelation or not, is incapable of understanding God or His wisdom. Because his heart is alienated from God, so that he does not love or do His will, his mind is darkened, and he cannot truly know God. Even when in Christ the light of God in its divine love shone upon men, they knew it not and saw no beauty in it.

In the epistle to the Romans, Paul dealt with man's trust in his own righteousness and its insufficiency. To the Corinthians, especially in the first three chapters, he exposes the insufficiency of man's wisdom with the Greeks and the Jews. Man was incapable of seeing the truth without a divine illumination, the light of the Holy Spirit.

The rulers of this world, Jew and Gentile, had crucified the Lord of glory because they did not know the wisdom of God. In writing to believers at Corinth, to warn them against the wisdom of the world, Paul is not dealing with any heresy, Jewish or heathen. He is speaking to believers who had fully accepted his gospel of a crucified Christ, but who were in danger of dealing with the truth in the power of human wisdom. He reminds them that the truth of God, as a hidden, spiritual mystery, can only be understood by a spiritual revelation.

God's Wisdom Versus Man's Wisdom

The rejection of Christ by the Jews had been the great proof of the incapacity of human wisdom to grasp a divine revelation without the spiritual illumination of the Holy Spirit. The Jews prided themselves on their attachment to God's Word, their study of it, and their conformity to it in life and conduct. The issue proved that they completely misunderstood it and rejected the very Messiah for whom they thought they were waiting.

Divine revelation, as Paul discusses it in this chapter, means three things. God must make known in His Word what He thinks and does. Every preacher who is to communicate the message must not only be in possession of the truth, but continually be taught by the Spirit how to speak it. And every hearer needs the inward illumination: it is only as he is a spiritual man, with his life under the rule of the Spirit, that his mind can take in spiritual truth. As we have the mind and attitudes of Christ, we can discern the truth as it is in Christ Jesus.

This teaching is what the Church and each

believer in our day especially needs. The need for the Holy Spirit's teaching is, in a general way, willingly admitted among most Christians. However, it will be found that neither in the teaching of the Church nor in the lives of believers does this blessed truth have practical and all-embracing supremacy. If the Holy Spirit's teaching is not supreme, the wisdom and the spirit of this world will still assert their power.

The proof of this will be found in what Paul says of his own preaching: "My preaching was not with enticing words of man's wisdom, but. . .in the Spirit; that your faith should not stand in the wisdom of men, but in the power of God." He is not writing about two gospels, but of two ways of preaching the one gospel of Christ's cross. He says that to preach it in persuasive words of man's wisdom produces a faith that will bear the mark of its origin. It will stand in the wisdom of man. As long as it is nourished by men and means, it may stand and flourish. But it cannot stand alone or in the day of trial. A man may, with such preaching, become a believer, but will be a weak believer.

On the other hand, the faith, begotten of preaching in the Spirit, stands in the power of God. The believer is led by the preaching, by the Holy Spirit Himself, past man, to direct contact with the living God: his faith stands in the power of God. The spiritual state of the great majority of our church members is weak and sickly, with little of the faith that stands in the power of God. The reason is because too much preaching is in the wisdom of man and not in the demonstration of the Spirit and of power. If a change is to be effected both in the spirit in which our preachers and teachers speak, and in the way our congregations listen and expect, it must begin in the personal life of the individual believer.

Crucify Your Own Wisdom

We must learn to fear our own wisdom. "Trust in the Lord with all thine heart; and lean not unto thine own understanding" (Proverbs 3:5). Paul says to believers: "If any man among you seemeth to be wise. . .let him become a fool, that he may be wise" (1 Corinthians 3:18). When Scripture tells us that "they that are Christ's have crucified the flesh" (Galatians 5:24), this includes the understanding of the flesh, the fleshly mind of which Scripture speaks. In the crucifixion of self, I give up my own goodness, my own strength, my own will because there is no good in it. I look to Christ by the power of His life to give me the goodness, the strength, and the will which is pleasing to God.

It must also be this way with my wisdom. Man's mind is one of his noblest and most God-like faculties. But sin rules over it and in it. A man may be truly converted and yet not know the extent to which his natural mind is trying to grasp and hold the truth of God. The reason that there is so much Bible reading and teaching which has no power to elevate and sanctify the life is simply this: it is not truth which has been revealed and received

185

through the Holy Spirit. This holds good, too, for truth which has once been taught us by the Holy Spirit, but which, having been lodged in the understanding, is now held simply by the memory.

Manna speedily loses its heavenliness when stored upon earth. Truth received from heaven loses its divine freshness unless there is the anointing with fresh oil every day. The believer must realize that there is nothing in which the power of the flesh can assert itself more than in the activity of the mind in its dealing with the divine Word. This will make him feel that he must continually seek, in Paul's language, "to become a fool." Each time he reads God's Word or thinks of God's truth he needs to wait in faith and teachableness for the promised teaching of the Spirit. He needs to ask for the circumcised ear: the ear in which the fleshly power of the understanding has been removed. Then the Spirit of the life in Christ Jesus within the heart can listen with the obedience of the life, even as Christ did. To such believers the word will be fulfilled: "I thank Thee, O Father. . .that Thou hast hid these things from the wise and prudent, and hast revealed them unto babes" (Luke 10:21).

The lesson for all ministers and teachers, all professors and theologians, all students and readers of the Bible, is one of deep and searching solemnity. I wish that over our theological seminaries and our training institutes these words of Paul were written: "God hath revealed them unto us by His Spirit" (1 Corinthians 2:10). Our ministers must train their congregations to see that it is not the amount, the clarity, or the interest of the Bible knowledge received that will decide the blessing and the power that it brings.

It is the measure of real dependence on the Holy Spirit that brings power and blessing, "them that honour Me I will honour" (1 Samuel 2:30). Nowhere will this word be found more true than here. The crucifixion of self and all its wisdom will most assuredly be met from above with the demonstration of the Spirit and of power.

A Christian can deceive himself with the appearance of wisdom in beautiful thoughts and sentiments, while the *power* of God is lacking. The *wisdom* of man stands in contrast to the power of God. The only true mark of divine wisdom is its power. The Kingdom of God is not words and thoughts and knowledge, but power. May God open our eyes to see how much of our religion consists in beautiful words, thoughts, and feelings, but *not in the power of God*.

It is not enough that the light of Christ shines on you in the Word. The light of the Spirit must shine in you. Each time you come to the Word in study, in hearing a sermon, or reading a religious book there ought to be a definite act of humility. You must deny your own wisdom and yield yourself in faith to the divine teacher. Believe very distinctly that He dwells within you. He seeks the mastery, the sanctification of your inner life, in entire surrender and obedience to Jesus. Rejoice to renew your surrender to Him.

Reject the spirit of the world still in you with its wisdom and self-confidence. Come, in poverty of spirit, to be led by the Spirit that is of God. "Be not conformed to this world: but be ye transformed by the renewing of your mind, that ye may prove what is that good, and acceptable, and perfect will of God" (Romans 12:2). The Spirit will teach a transformed, renewed life that only wants to know God's perfect will. Deny your own fleshly wisdom. Wait for the wisdom in the inward parts which God has promised. You will increasingly be able to testify of the things which have not entered into the hearts of men and will understand "God hath revealed them to us by His Spirit."

Prayer

O Lord, teach Your Church that wherever Christ as the power of God is not manifested, it is because He is so little known as the wisdom of God. Teach Your Church to lead each child of God to the personal teaching and revelation of Christ within. Show us, O God, that the one great hindrance is our own wisdom, our imagining that we can understand the Word and truth of God. Teach us to become fools that we may be wise. May our whole life become one continued act of faith, that the Holy Spirit will surely do His work of teaching, guiding, and leading into the truth. We wait for this. Amen.

Chapter 23

THE SPIRIT AND THE FLESH

"Are ye so foolish? having begun in the Spirit, are ye now made perfect by the flesh?"—Galatians 3:3.

"We are the circumcision, which worship God in the spirit, and rejoice in Christ Jesus, and have no confidence in the flesh. Though I might also have confidence in the flesh"—Philippians 3:3,4.

The flesh is the name by which Scripture designates our fallen nature—soul and body. The soul at creation was placed between the spiritual and the worldly to guide them into that perfect union which would result in man attaining his destiny, a spiritual body.

When the soul yielded to the temptation of the senses, it broke away from the rule of the Spirit and came under the power of the body—it became flesh. And now the flesh is not only without the Spirit, but even hostile to it: "the flesh lusteth against the Spirit" (Galatians 5:17).

In this antagonism of the flesh to the Spirit,

there are two sides. On the one hand, the flesh lusts against the Spirit in its committing sin and transgressing God's law. On the other hand, its hostility to the Spirit is shown no less in its seeking to serve God and do His will. In yielding to the flesh, the soul sought itself instead of seeking God to whom the Spirit linked it. Selfishness prevailed over God's will. Selfishness became its ruling principle.

This spirit of self is so subtle and mighty in sinning against God, that, even when the soul learns to serve God, it still asserts its power and refuses to let the Spirit lead alone. In its efforts to be religious, it is still the great enemy that hinders and quenches the Spirit. This deceitfulness of the flesh often causes the same problem Paul found among the Galatians: "Having begun in the Spirit, are ye now made perfect by the flesh?" The surrender to the Spirit must be complete and maintained by waiting on Him in dependence and humility. If this is not done, then what the Spirit has begun very quickly passes over into confidence in the flesh.

Satan's Device

The remarkable thing is that when the flesh seeks to serve God, it becomes the strength of sin. The Pharisees, with their self-righteousness and carnal religion, fell into pride and selfishness and became the servants of sin. The works of the flesh were so manifest among the Galatians that they were in danger of devouring one another.

This is Satan's most crafty device for keeping souls in bondage—inciting them to a religion in the flesh. He knows that the power of the flesh can never please God or conquer sin. He knows that in due time the flesh that has gained supremacy over the Spirit in the service of God will assert and maintain that same supremacy in the service of sin.

It is only where the Spirit truly has the entire rule in the life of worship that He will have the power to lead in the life of practical obedience. If I am to deny self in communicating with men, to conquer selfishness and temper, I must first learn to deny self in communicating with God. The soul, the seat of self, must learn to bow to the Spirit where God dwells.

The contrast between the worship in the Spirit and the trusting in the flesh is very beautifully expressed in Paul's description of the true circumcision—the circumcision of the heart—whose praise is not of men, but of God: "Which worship God in the Spirit, and rejoice in Christ Jesus, and have no confidence in the flesh" (Philippians 3:3). Placing Christ Jesus in the center, Paul marks on the one hand the great danger of worship and on the other the safeguard by which its full enjoyment is secured. Confidence in the flesh is the one thing above all others that does not render glory to Christ Jesus. Worship by the Spirit is the one thing that alone can make it indeed life and truth. May the Spirit reveal to us what it is thus to glory in Christ Jesus!

All history and experience teach us that there is a glorying in Christ Jesus that is accompanied by much confidence in the flesh. This was true with the Galatians. The teachers whom Paul opposed so earnestly were all preachers of Christ and His cross. They preached as those who had the beginnings of God's Spirit, but they had allowed their own wisdom and their own thoughts to say what the cross meant. They had reconciled the cross to a religion which was legal and carnal.

The mistake of the Galatian church is repeated to this day even in the churches that are most confidently assured that they are free from Galatian error. Just notice how often the doctrine of justification by faith is spoken of as if that were the chief teaching of the Galatian epistle. The doctrine of the Holy Spirit's indwelling as received by faith and our walking by the Spirit is hardly mentioned.

No Confidence In The Flesh

Christ crucified is the wisdom of God. The confidence in the flesh, in connection with the glorying in Christ, is seen in confidence in its own wisdom. Scripture is studied, preached, heard, and believed in the power of the natural mind with little insistence upon the absolute need for the Spirit's personal teaching. It is seen in the absolute confidence with which men know that they have the truth, though they have it far more from human than divine teaching. It is seen in the absence of that teachable attitude that waits for

God to reveal His truth in His own light.

Christ, through the Holy Spirit, is not only the wisdom but the power of God. The confidence in the flesh, along with much glorying in Christ Jesus, is to be seen and felt in much of the work of the Christian Church. Human effort and human arrangement take a much larger place than the waiting on the power that comes from on high.

Much unsuccessful effort can be traced to this one evil that is found in the larger ecclesiastical organizations, in individual churches, and in the inner life of Christians. There is no lack of acknowledging Christ, His person and work, as our only hope. There is no lack of giving Him the glory. And yet so much confidence in the flesh makes the results ineffective.

Christ is the wisdom and the power of God. The root of all trust in our own strength is trust in our own wisdom, the idea that we know how to serve God because we have His Word. This wisdom of man, in his accepting God's Word, is the greatest danger of the Church. Man's wisdom is the secret and most subtle form in which we are led to perfect in the flesh what was begun in the Spirit.

Our only safety is the Holy Spirit. The path of safety is a great willingness to be taught by Him and a holy fear of walking after the flesh in the least thing. It is a loving surrender in everything to the obedience to which Christ promises the Spirit. Along with all this, it is the living faith that the Spirit will, in divine power, possess our life and live it for us.

There are many, striving earnestly for a life in the fullness of consecration and the fullness of blessing, who will find here the secret of failure. One of my first purposes and most earnest prayers in writing this book has been to help those people.

Perhaps the fullness of Jesus was opened up to them in a sermon or speech, in a book or conversation or private prayer with the possibility of a holy life in Him. The believer then felt it was all so beautiful and so simple that nothing could keep it back any longer. And perhaps, as he accepted what was seen to be so sure and so near, he entered into an enjoyment and experienced a power before unknown.

But it did not last. There was a worm at its root. The search for the reason for this was vain. Frequently, the only possible answer was that the surrender was not entire or faith's acceptance not perfect. And yet the believer felt sure that he was ready to give up all. He longed to let Jesus have all and to trust Him for all.

Listen to the blessed teaching of God's Word. It was the confidence in the flesh that spoiled your glorying in Christ Jesus. It was self doing what the Spirit alone can do. It was the soul taking the lead, in the hope that the Spirit would consent to its efforts, instead of trusting the Holy Spirit to lead and do all. It was following Jesus without the denial of self. This was the secret trouble.

Come and listen to Paul as he tells of the only safeguard against this danger: "We are the circumcision, which worship God in the spirit, and rejoice in Christ Jesus, and have no confidence in the flesh." Here are the two elements of spiritual worship. The Spirit exalts Jesus and abases the flesh. If we want to truly glory in Jesus and have Him glorified in us, we must simply learn what this worship of God by the Spirit is.

Let us try to fully realize that there are two life-giving principles of man's life. In most Christians, there is a mixed life, yielding now to the one and then to the other. God's will is that we *never* walk after the flesh. He wants us to walk after the Spirit. Let us accept God's will. The Holy Spirit has been given to bring our life into conformity with it. May God show us how the Holy Spirit can become a new life in us, revealing Christ as our life. Then we can say, it is no longer I that live, "but Christ liveth in me" (Galatians 2:20).

Glory In Jesus

I can only repeat, once again, the purpose of this whole book—*glory in Christ Jesus*. Glory in Him as the glorified One who baptizes with the Holy Spirit. In great simplicity and restfulness believe in Him as having given His own Spirit within you. Believe in that gift. Believe in the Holy Spirit dwelling within you. Accept this as the secret of the life of Christ in you. The Holy Spirit is dwelling in the hidden recesses of your spirit. Meditate on it. Believe Jesus and His Word concerning it until your soul bows with holy fear and awe before God under the glory of the truth: the

Holy Spirit of God is indeed dwelling in me.

Yield yourself to His leading. We have seen that leading is not just in the mind or thoughts but in life and attitude. Yield yourself to God to be guided by the Holy Spirit in all your conduct. He is promised to those who love Jesus and obey Him. Do not be afraid to say He knows that you do love and do obey Him with your whole heart. Remember, then, what the one central object of His coming was: to restore the departed Lord Jesus to His disciples.

I cannot glory in a distant Jesus from whom I am separated. When I try to do it, it is a thing of effort, and I must have the help of the flesh to do it. I can only *truly glory* in a present Savior, whom the Holy Spirit glorifies and reveals in His glory within me. As He does this, the flesh is abased and kept in its place of crucifixion as an accursed thing. As He does it, the deeds of the flesh are made to die. Then my whole religion will be: having no confidence in the flesh, glorying in Christ Jesus, and worshipping by the Spirit of God.

Having begun in the Spirit, continue, go on, persevere in the Spirit. Beware of, for one single moment, continuing or perfecting the work of the Spirit in the flesh. Let "no confidence in the flesh" be your battle cry. Let a deep distrust of the flesh and fear of grieving the Spirit by walking after the flesh keep you very low and humble before God. Ask God for the Spirit of revelation that you may see how Jesus is all and does all. The Holy Spirit will indeed take the place of your life, and Jesus will be enthroned as the keeper, guide, and life of your soul.

Prayer

Teach us to know how the flesh can be conquered and its power broken. In the death of Your beloved Son, our old nature has been crucified. May we consider all things as loss to be made conformable to that death, and may we have the old nature kept in the place of death. We yield ourselves to the leading and rule of Your Holy Spirit. We believe that Christ is our life through the Spirit, so that, instead of the life of effort and work, an entirely new life works within us. Our Father, by faith we give up all to Your Spirit to be our life in us. Amen.

Chapter 24

ARE YOU SPIRITUAL OR CARNAL?

"And I, brethren, could not speak unto you as unto spiritual, but as unto carnal, as unto babes in Christ. I have fed you with milk and not with meat: for hitherto ye were not able to bear it, neither yet now are ye able. . .for whereas there is among you envying, and strife, and divisions, are ye not carnal, and walk as men?"—1 Corinthians 3:1-3.

"If we live by the Spirit, let us also walk in the Spirit"—Galatians 5:25.

In the previous chapter, Paul contrasted the believer as spiritual with the unregenerate as the natural (or physical) man. He contrasted the man of the Spirit with the man of the soul (see 1 Corinthians 2:14,15). He supplements that teaching by telling the Corinthians that though they have the Spirit, he cannot call them spiritual.

The word *spiritual* belongs to those who have not only received the Spirit, but have yielded themselves to Him to possess and rule their whole life. Those who have not done this, in whom the power of the flesh is still more manifest than that of the Spirit, must not be called spiritual, but fleshly or carnal.

There are thus three states in which a man may be found. The unregenerate is still *the natural man,* not having the Spirit of God. The regenerate, who is still a babe in Christ, is *the carnal man,* giving way to the power of the flesh. The believer in whom the Spirit has obtained full supremacy is *the spiritual man.* This whole passage from Corinthians is suggestive of rich instruction in regard to the life of the Spirit within us.

The Carnal Christian

The young Christian is still carnal. Regeneration is a birth. The center and root of the personality, the spirit, has been renewed and taken possession of by the Spirit of God. But time is needed for this power to extend from that center through all of our being. The Kingdom of God is like a seed. The life in Christ is a growth.

It would be against the laws of nature and grace alike if we expected from the babe the strength that can only be found in mature Christians. Even where there is great singleness of heart and love for the Savior in the young convert, time is needed for a deeper knowledge of self and sin. He needs to gain spiritual insight into what God's will and grace are.

It is not unnatural that the emotions are deeply stirred with the young believer and that the mind delights in the contemplation of divine truth.

With the growth in grace, the will becomes the more important thing. The waiting for the Spirit's power in the life and character becomes more important than those thoughts and images of the life which the mind alone could give. We do not need to wonder if the babe in Christ is still carnal.

Many Christians remain carnal. God has not only called us to grow, but He has provided all the conditions and powers necessary for growth. Yet, it is sadly true that there are many Christians who, like the Corinthians, remain babes in Christ when they ought to be going on to perfection. In some cases, the blame is almost more with the Church and its teaching than with the individuals themselves. When preaching emphasizes the pardon and peace of salvation, or when the truth of the Holy Spirit's indwelling is not taught clearly, growth can hardly be expected. The causes of evil are ignorance of God's power and defective human views of the gospel of salvation.

In other cases the root of the evil is to be found in the unwillingness of the Christian to deny self and crucify the flesh. Jesus asks each disciple to deny self and follow Him. The Spirit is only given to the obedient. He can only do His work in those who are absolutely willing to give up self to the death. The sin that proved that the Corinthians were carnal was their jealousy and strife.

When Christians are not willing to give up the sin of selfishness, they are carnal. When, in the home or in the wider circle of church and public life, they want to retain the freedom of excusing evil feelings they are carnal. If they pronounce their own judgments and speak words that are not in perfect love, then they remain carnal. With all their knowledge, their enjoyment of religious ordinances, and their work for God's Kingdom, they remain carnal and not spiritual. They grieve the Holy Spirit of God. They cannot have the assurance and testimony that they are pleasing to God.

The carnal Christian cannot understand spiritual truth. Paul writes to these Corinthians: "I have fed you with milk, and not with meat; for ye were not able to bear it neither yet now are ye able." The Corinthians prided themselves on their wisdom. There was nothing in Christ's teaching that they would not have been able to understand. But the Holy Spirit can only give the real spiritual entering into the truth in power, so as to possess it and be possessed by it. He gives it only to the spiritually-minded man. The teaching and leading of the Spirit is given to the obedient and is preceded by the dominion of the Spirit over the body. (See Romans 8:13,14).

Spiritual knowledge is not deep thought, but living contact, entering into spiritual reality in Jesus. "The Holy Ghost teacheth; comparing spiritual things with spiritual" (1 Corinthians 2:13). He works spiritual truth in a spiritual mind. It is not the power of intellect, it is not even the earnest desire to know the truth, that equips a man for the Spirit's teaching. It is a life yielded to Him in waiting dependence and full obedience to be made spiritual that receives spiritual wisdom and understanding.

It is easy to understand how a carnal or fleshly life with its actions, and the fleshly mind with its knowledge, act and react on each other. As long as we are giving way to the flesh, we are incapable of receiving spiritual insight into truth. We may "understand all mysteries, and all knowledge" (1 Corinthians 13:2). But without love—the love which the Spirit works in the inner life—it is only a knowledge which puffs up. It profits nothing. The carnal life makes the knowledge carnal.

This knowledge, held in the fleshly mind, strengthens the religion of the flesh, of self-trust and self-effort. The truth so received has no power to renew and make free. No wonder there is so much Bible teaching and Bible knowledge with so little real spiritual results of holiness. Unless we are living spiritual lives full of humility, love, and self-sacrifice, spiritual truth—the truth of God—cannot enter or profit us.

The Spiritual Christian

Every Christian is called of God to be a spiritual man. The Corinthians were recently brought out of gross unbelief, yet Paul reproves them for not yet being spiritual. The great redemption in Christ had this as its distinct purpose: the removal of every hindrance so that the Spirit of God might be able to make man's heart and life a worthy home for God who is a Spirit. That redemption was no failure.

The Holy Spirit came down to inaugurate a new

outpouring of indwelling life and power that was before unknown. This was made possible by the love of the Father, the power of the Son, and the presence of the Spirit on earth. Just as the natural man can become a regenerate man, a regenerate man, who is still carnal, can become spiritual.

When a man is first regenerated, the new life within him is only a small seed in the midst of a great body of sin and flesh with its fleshly wisdom and will. In that little seed there is Christ and His Spirit as an almighty power. But it is such a little, feeble thing that it is easily overlooked or distrusted. Faith knows the mighty power there is in that little seed to overcome the world and bring the flesh and life into subjection. So the Spirit rules and conquers and makes the deeds of the body die, and the man becomes truly spiritual.

It is the Holy Spirit who makes the spiritual man. He alone can do it. He does it most certainly where the whole man is yielded up to Him. The whole being is influenced and sanctified by the Holy Spirit. First our spirit, then the soul—the will, the feelings, the mind—is sanctified. Finally, the body is brought under His control when all three are moved and guided by Him. This makes and marks the spiritual man.

True spiritual insight into God's Word depends upon a spiritual life. This is an important lesson for all ministers and teachers of the Word. Let us pray for all the leaders of the Church that they may be spiritual men. It is not the soundness of the teaching itself, nor the earnestness of the teacher, that is essential. It is the power of the Spirit, making the teacher's life, thoughts, and words truly spiritual, that secures the blessing.

We must seek the deep, living, absorbing conviction that there is a Holy Spirit in us. We must believe that He is the mighty power of God dwelling and working within us. We must see Him as the representative of Jesus, making Him present within us as our redeemer King, mighty to save. The Holy Spirit has His home within us. In our spirit is His hidden, blessed dwelling place.

However, we find that there is an opposing power in the flesh. From Scripture we learn how the flesh has its twofold action: from the flesh springs not only unrighteousness, but self-righteousness. Both must be confessed and surrendered to Him whom the Spirit would reveal and enthrone as Lord, our mighty Savior.

All that is carnal and sinful, all the works of the flesh, must be given up and cast out. Also, all that is carnal (however religious it appears), all confidence in the flesh, all self-effort and self-struggling must be rooted out. The soul, with its power, must be brought into the captivity and subjection of Jesus Christ. In deep and daily dependence on God, the Holy Spirit must be accepted, waited for, and followed.

By walking in faith and obedience, we may count on the Holy Spirit to do a divine and most blessed work within us. "If we live by the Spirit"—this is the faith that is needed. If we believe that God's Spirit dwells in us, "let us also walk in the Spirit." This is the obedience that God requires. By faith in the Holy Spirit who is in us, we have sufficient strength to walk by the Spirit and yield ourselves to His mighty power. Then, He can work in us to will and to do all that is pleasing in God's sight.

Prayer

Gracious God, let us hear Your call to be spiritual. Strengthen our faith, that we may be filled with the confidence that the Holy Spirit will do His work to make us spiritual. We desire to cease from self and doubt. We give ourselves to Jesus our Lord to rule in us, to reveal Himself by the Spirit. We bow before You in the childlike faith that Your Spirit, the Spirit of God, dwells in us every moment. May our souls increasingly be filled with holy awe and reverence at His presence. Grant that we may be mightily strengthened by Him in the inner man. Then we shall be truly spiritual. Amen.

Chapter 25

YOU ARE THE TEMPLE OF
THE HOLY SPIRIT

*"Know ye not that ye are the temple of God,
and that the Spirit of God dwelleth in you?"*—1
Corinthians 3:16.

In using the illustration of the temple as the
type of God's dwelling in us by the Holy Spirit,
Scripture invites us to study this analogy. The temple was made in all things according to a pattern
seen by Moses. One of the realities symbolized by
the temple is man's threefold nature. Because man
was created in the image of God, the temple
requested the mystery of man's approach into the
presence of God. It also represents God's way of
entering into man, to take up His abode with him.

We are familiar with the division of the temple
into three parts. There was its exterior, seen by all
men, with the *Outer Court,* into which every
Israelite could enter. All the external religious services were performed there. Next, was the *Holy
Place,* into which alone the priests might enter, to
present to God the blood or the incense, the bread

or the oil.

Although near, they were still not within the veil. They were not to come into the immediate presence of God. God dwelt in the *Holy of Holies,* in a light inaccesible, where none might venture. The momentary entering of the high priest once a year brought into full consciousness the truth that there was no place for man there, until the veil would be torn and taken away.

Body, Soul, And Spirit

Man is God's temple. In him, too, there are the three parts. In the *body* you have the Outer Court, the external visible life. In our body all conduct has to be regulated by God's law and all service is done without us and for us to bring us near to God. Then there is *the soul,* with its inner life, its power of mind and feeling and will. In the regenerate man, this is the Holy Place. There, the soul's thoughts and desires move to and fro as the priests of the sanctuary, rendering God their service. Then comes within the veil, hidden from all human sight and light, the hidden, innermost sanctuary, "the secret place of the Most High" (Psalm 91:1). This is where God dwells and where man may not enter until the veil is torn at God's own bidding.

Man does not only have body and soul, but also *spirit.* Deeper down than where the soul with its consciousness can enter, there is a spirit-nature linking man with God. So fearful is sin's power, that in some this power is given up as dead. They are sensual, not having the Spirit. In others, it is nothing more than a dormant power, a possibility waiting for the quickening of the Holy Spirit. In the believer it is the inner chamber of the heart which the Spirit has taken possession of. He waits to do His glorious work, making soul and body holy to the Lord.

This indwelling, unless it is recognized, yielded to, and humbly maintained in adoration and love, often brings comparatively little blessing. The one great lesson, which the truth that we are God's temple must teach us, is this—to acknowledge the Holy Presence that dwells within us. This alone will enable us to regard the whole temple, even the Outer Court, as sacred to His service and to yield every power of our nature to His leading and will.

The most sacred part of the temple, that for which all the rest existed and on which all depended, was the Holiest of All. Even though the priests might never enter and see the glory that dwelt there, all their conduct was regulated and their faith was inspired by the thought of the unseen Presence there.

It was this that gave the sprinkling of the blood and the burning of the incense their value. It was the Most Holy, the Holiest of All, that made the place of their serving a Holy Place to them. Their whole life was controlled and inspired by the faith of the unseen indwelling glory within the veil.

It is the same with the believer. He must learn by faith that he is God's temple, because God's

Spirit dwells in him. Then, he can yield himself to his calling with reverence and confidence. As long as he looks only into the Holy Place, into the heart, he will often search in vain for the Holy Spirit. He will only find cause for bitter shame that his workings are so few and weak.

Each of us must learn to know that there is a Holiest of All in that temple which we are. The secret place of the Most High within us must become the central truth in our temple worship. This must be to us the meaning of our confession: "I believe in the Holy Spirit."

The Holiest Of All

How is this deep faith in the hidden indwelling to become ours? Taking our stand upon God's blessed Word, we must accept and appropriate its teaching. We must take trouble to believe that God means what it says. I am a temple, just like the temple God commanded to be built in Israel. He meant me to see in it what I am to be. There the Holiest of All was the central point, the essential thing. It was all dark, secret, and hidden, until the time of unveiling came. It demands and received the faith of priest and people.

The Holiest of All within me, too, is unseen and hidden, a thing for faith alone to know and accept. Let me, as I approach the Holy One, bow before Him in deep and lowly reverence. Let me there say that I believe what God says, that His Holy Spirit even now has His abode within me. I will meditate and be still, until something of the overwhelming glory of this truth comes upon me.

Then, by faith, I will begin to realize—I am His temple, and, in the secret place, He sits upon His throne. As I yield myself in silent meditation and worship day by day, surrendering my whole being to Him, He will shine into my heart the light of His presence.

As this thought fills the heart, the faith of the indwelling, hidden presence will influence. The Holy Place will be ruled from the Most Holy. All the thoughts and feelings of the soul will come and surrender themselves to the Holy Power that sits within on the throne. Amid the terrible experience of failure and sin a new hope will dawn.

Though I tried very hard, I could not keep the Holy Place for God, because I did not know that He kept the Most Holy for Himself. If I give Him there the glory due His name, in the holy worship of the inner temple, He will send forth His light and His truth throughout my being. Through my mind and will He will reveal His power to sanctify and bless. Through the soul, coming more mightily under His rule, His power will work out even into my body.

With passions and appetites, with every thought brought into subjection, the hidden Holy Spirit will penetrate deeper into the body through the soul. Through the Spirit, the deeds of the body will be made dead. The river of water that flows from under the throne of God and the Lamb will go through all the outer nature with its cleansing and quickening power.

Believe that you are the temple of the living God and that the Spirit of God dwells in you! You have been sealed with the Holy Spirit. He is the mark, the living assurance of your sonship and your Father's love. If this up to now has been a thought that has brought you little comfort, see if the reason is not here. You sought for Him in the Holy Place amid the powers and services of your inner life which come within your vision. And you could hardly discern Him there. And so you could not appropriate the comfort and strength the Comforter was meant to bring.

Do not look there but look down deeper in the secret place of the Most High, there you will find Him. There faith will find Him. And as faith worships in holy reverence before the Father, wait in holy stillness on God to grant you the mighty power of His Spirit. Wait in holy stillness for the Spirit and be assured He will arise and fill His temple with His glory.

Remember, the veil was only for a time. When the preparation was complete, the veil of the flesh was torn. You must yield your soul's inner life to the innermost life of the Spirit. Then as the traffic between the Most Holy and the Holy One becomes more true and unbroken, the fullness will come in your soul. In the power of Him in whom the veil was torn, there will come to you an experience in which the veil will be taken away. Then the Most Holy and the Holy One will become one in your new life. The hidden glory of the secret place will stream into your daily life. The service of the Holy

Place will be in the power of the eternal Spirit.

Let us fall down and worship! "Be silent, O all flesh, before the Lord: for He is raised up out of His holy habitation" (Zechariah 2:13).

Prayer

Lord God, I do now accept the blessed truth: God the Spirit, the Holy Spirit, who is God Almighty, dwells in me. Blessed Jesus, I yield my whole being to You. I trust You to rise up in power and have dominion within me. Blessed Spirit, You are within me. On You do I wait all the day. I belong to You. Take entire possession of me for the Father and the Son. Amen.

Chapter 26

RECEIVE THE SPIRIT THROUGH FAITH

"Christ hath redeemed us from the curse of the law. . . .that the blessing of Abraham might come upon the Gentiles through Christ Jesus; that we might receive the promise of the Spirit through faith"—Galatians 3:13,14.

In Scripture, the word *faith* is used the first time in connection with Abraham. The secret of his strength for obedience, and what made him so pleasing to God, was that he believed God. He became the father of all who believe. He also became the great example of the blessing which divine favor bestows and the path in which it comes. God proved Himself to Abraham as the God who quickens the dead. He does this in fuller measure for us, too, by giving us the Spirit of His own divine life to dwell in us. Just as this quickening power came to Abraham through faith, so the blessing of Abraham, and the promise of the Spirit, is made ours by faith.

All the lessons of Abraham's life center in this: "We receive the promise of the Spirit through faith." If we want to know what the faith is through which the Spirit is received, and how that faith comes and grows, we must study what God has taught us about it in Abraham's story.

We see what faith is in Abraham's life. Faith is the spiritual sense by which man recognizes and accepts the revelation of his God—a spiritual sense awakened by that revelation. Because God has chosen Abraham and determined to reveal Himself, Abraham became a man of faith. Each new revelation was an act of the divine will. It is the divine will and the revelation in which it carries out its purpose that is the cause and the life of faith. The more distinct the revelation or contact with God, the deeper faith is stirred in the soul.

Paul speaks of "trust in the living God" (1 Timothy 4:10). It is only as God draws close and touches the soul that living faith will be activated. Faith is not an independent act by which we take what God says in our own strength. Nor is it an entirely passive state in which we believe that God will do with us what He will. Rather, it is the receptive soul that causes us to yield ourselves and accept His Word and His working in and through us. It is when the soul is receptive that God comes close and touches us with His power.

Faith Like Abraham's

It is very evident that faith has two things to deal with: *the presence* and *the Word* of the Lord. Only the living presence makes the Word come alive in power. There is much reading and preaching of the Word that bears little fruit, so much straining and praying for faith with little result. Men deal with the Word more than with the living God.

Faith has truly been defined as "taking God at His word." For many people this has only meant taking the Word as God's. They did not see the force of the thought, taking God at His word. A key or a door handle has no value until I use it for the lock and the door I want to open. It is only in direct and living contact with God Himself that the Word will open the heart to believe.

Faith takes God at His word. It can only do this when and as He gives Himself. I may have all God's precious promises presented clearly in the Bible. I may have perfectly learned to understand that I have to trust the promise to have it fulfilled. Yet, I may not find the longed-for blessing. The faith that comes at the time of inheritance is the attitude of soul which waits for God Himself. It waits first to speak His Word to me and then to do the thing He has spoken.

Faith is fellowship with God. Faith is surrender to God. Faith is the impression made by His drawing near. It is the possession *He takes* of the soul by His Word, holding and preparing it for His work. Once it has been awakened, it watches for every appearing of the divine will. It listens for and accepts every indication of the divine presence. It looks for and expects the fulfillment of every divine promise.

Such was the faith through which Abraham inherited the promises. Such is the faith by which the blessing of Abraham comes upon the Gentiles in Christ Jesus and by which we thus receive the promise of the Spirit. In all our study of the work of the Holy Spirit and of the way in which He comes, let us hold to this word: "We receive the promise of the Spirit through faith."

The believer may be striving for the full consciousness that the Spirit dwells within or for a deeper assurance of His shedding abroad of God's love in the heart. He may desire a clearer experience of the Spirit's guiding into all truth, or he may long for the endowment of power to labor and to bless.

Whatever his needs, let him remember that the law of faith demands this application: "According to your faith be it unto you" (Matthew 9:29). We receive the promise of the Spirit by faith. Let us seek for Abraham's blessing with Abraham's faith.

Let our faith in this matter begin where his began: in meeting God and waiting on God. "The Lord appeared unto Abram. . . .And Abram fell on his face: and God talked with him" (Genesis 17:1,3). Let us look up to our God and Father as the living God to fill us with His Holy Spirit. The blessing He has for us is the same He gave to Abraham, only larger, fuller, and more wonderful. To Abraham, He came as the life-giving God. "He believed, even God, who quickeneth the dead" (Romans 4:17). "Abraham. . .offered up Isaac. . .accounting that God was able to raise him up" (Hebrews 11:17,19).

To read and think, to long and pray, to consecrate ourselves and grasp the promise, to hold fast the blessed truth that the Spirit dwells with us—all this is good in its place, but it does not bring the blessing. The one essential thing is to have the heart filled with faith in the living God. In that faith, we are to abide in living contact with Him, and in that faith we are to wait and worship before His Holy Presence. In such fellowship with God, the Holy Spirit fills the heart.

Maintaining Your Faith

When we have taken up this position of faith, let us maintain it. We are then in the right state for the Spirit to further reveal what God has prepared for us. As we are convicted of our need for the Spirit, we will be kept in that humbling sense of dependence out of which childlike trust is most surely begotten. We will be preserved from that life of strain and effort which has often led to failure.

We failed because, in the very attempt to serve God in the Spirit, we were seeking confidence in the flesh. The deep undertone of our life in listening to the Word will be the assurance that overtowers every other certainty: "much more shall the heavenly Father give the Holy Spirit to them that ask Him" (Luke 11:13).

Such a faith will not be without its trials. Isaac, the God-given, faith-accepted life of Isaac, had to be given up to death that it might be received back as life from the dead. The God-given experience of the Spirit's working passes away many times and leaves the soul apparently dull and dead. This is only until we learn that a living faith can rejoice in a living God, even when all feeling and experience appear to contradict the promise. The life of Christ is revealed as His death works in us and as in weakness and nothingness we look to Him.

We receive the promise of the Spirit through faith. As faith grows larger and broader, the receiving of the promised Spirit will be fuller and deeper. Each new revelation of God to Abraham made his faith stronger and his acquaintance with God more intimate. When his God drew near, he knew what to expect. Abraham knew to trust Him even in the most unlikely appearances.

Faith is the one thing that pleases God. In all worship and work that is acceptable to God in Christ Jesus, it is faith that receives the testimony that we are pleasing to Him. Why? Because faith goes out of self, gives God alone the glory, only looks to God's Son, and is receptive of God's Spirit. Faith is not merely the positive conviction that God's Word or promise is true, because we may even have this confidence in the power of the flesh.

Faith is the spiritual vehicle of the soul through which it waits on the living God, listens to Him, takes His words from Himself, and has communion with Him. As this habit of soul is cultivated, as the whole life we live is by faith, the Spirit can enter freely and flow fully.

If you long for the power of the Holy Spirit to reveal Jesus as the ever-present Savior from sin, all you need to do is believe. Begin each day with a quiet act of meditation and faith. In quiet reflection, turn inward, not to see the work the Holy Spirit does, but to yield your spirit to Him who dwells there in secret.

Say in deep humility: "I have within me, small and hidden, the seed of the Kingdom, the seed of eternal life. I have found the seed of the living Word, the seed of God, within me. I know now where it dwells." Bow before God in fear and trembling because He works in you, and let faith take time before Him to become confident that "I have the Holy Spirit within me this day."

Prayer

Our Holy God, draw us mightily into Your Holy Presence and keep us waiting there. Deliver us from the terrible fascination with the world and the flesh so that Your divine glory may be our all-absorbing desire. May our whole heart be emptied to receive the Holy Spirit's revelation of Christ within. We desire to take Your words and let them dwell richly in us.

We desire in stillness of soul to be silent unto God and wait for Him. We desire to trust and believe that the Father has given us His Spirit within us and is in secret working to reveal His Son. We do live the life of faith. We do believe in the Holy Spirit. Amen.

Chapter 27

THE SPIRIT OF LOVE

"The fruit of the Spirit is love"—Galatians 5:22.

"I beseech you. . .for the love of the Spirit"—Romans 15:30.

"Who also declared unto us your love in the Spirit"—Colossians 1:8.

These verses lead us up into the very center of the inner sanctuary. We will have to learn that love is not only one of the fruits of the Spirit, but it is the most important of all. The Spirit is nothing less than divine love come down to dwell in us. We have only as much of the Spirit as we have of love.

God is Spirit. God is love. In these two words, we have the only attempt that Scripture makes to give us a definition of God. As a Spirit, He has life in Himself and is independent of all around Him. He has the power to penetrate with His own life and to communicate Himself. It is through the Spirit that God is the Father of spirits. He is the God of creation and is the God and redeemer of man.

All life is owing to the Spirit of God. This is so because God is love. He is love as seen in the Father giving all He has to the Son and the Son seeking all He has in the Father. In this life of love between the Father and the Son, the Spirit is the bond of fellowship. The Father is the loving One, the fountain. The Son is the beloved One, the great reservoir of love, always receiving and giving back. The Spirit is the living love that makes them one. In Him the divine life of love has its ceaseless flow and overflowing.

That same love with which the Father loves the Son rests on us and seeks to fill us, too. It is through the Spirit that this love of God is revealed and communicated to us. It was the Spirit that led Jesus to the work of love for which He was anointed—to preach glad tidings to the poor and deliverance to the captives. Through that same Spirit He offered Himself as a sacrifice for us. The Spirit comes to us with all the love of God and of Jesus. The Spirit is the love of God.

When that Spirit enters us, His first work is: "the love of God is shed abroad in our hearts by the Holy Ghost which is given unto us" (Romans 5:5). What He gives is not only the faith or the experience of how greatly God loves, but something infinitely more glorious. The love of God, as a spiritual existence and a living power, enters our hearts. It cannot be otherwise, because the love of God exists in the Spirit.

The outpouring of the Spirit is the inpouring of

love. This love now possesses the heart. That same love with which God loves Jesus, ourselves, and all His children overflows from us to all the world. If we trust and yield to this love, it will be power for us to live, too. The Spirit is the life of the love of God. The Spirit in us is the love of God taking up abode within us.

Love And Our Spirit

Such is the relationship between the Spirit and the love of God. Let us now consider the relationship between our spirit and love. We must here again refer to what has been said of man's threefold nature—body, soul, and spirit.

We saw how the soul, as the seat of self-consciousness, was created to be subject to the spirit, the seat of God-consciousness. We learned how sin was simply the asserting of self. It was the soul refusing the rule of the spirit in order to gratify itself in the lust of the body. The fruit of that sin was that self ascended the throne of the soul to rule there instead of God in the spirit.

Selfishness thus became the ruling power in man's life. The self that refused God His right at the same time refused fellowman what was due him. The terrible story of sin in the world is simply the history of the origin, the growth, the power, and the reign of self. The original order is restored when the soul gives the spirit the precedence it claims and self is denied to make way for God. Then, selfishness will be conquered and love toward our brother will flow from love toward

God. In other words, the renewed spirit must become the dwelling place of the Spirit of God and His love. Then, the regenerate man will yield himself to let the Spirit have His way, and love will again become our life and our joy.

To every disciple the Master says, "let him deny himself. . .and follow Me" (Mark 8:34). Many have sought in vain to follow Jesus in His life of love and could not, because they have neglected what was essential—denying self. When self is not denied but follows Jesus, it always fails. It cannot love as He loves.

If we understand this, we are prepared to admit that our proof of discipleship is love. The change we profess to have undergone is divine. The deliverance from the power of self and sin is complete. The indwelling of the Spirit of God's love is real and true. These make it possible for us to live a life of love that fulfills the law.

Love should be the natural overflow of the new life in every believer. The fact that this is not so is simply another proof of how believers do not understand their calling to walk after the Spirit and really be spiritual men.

Instead, we complain about our unconquered tempers and our selfishness. We complain about harsh judgments and unkind words, about the lack of Christlike meekness and patience and gentleness. We criticize the little that is being done by the majority of Christians in the way of self-sacrifice for the social and religious needs of the perishing world around them.

All this is simply proof that it has not yet been understood that to be a Christian means to have the Spirit of Christ. Being a Christian means to be a fountain of His love springing up and flowing out in streams of living water. We do not know what the Spirit is meant to be in us, because we have not accepted Him for the reason the Master gave Him. We are more carnal than spiritual.

It was thus with the *Corinthians*. In them, we see the remarkable phenomenon of a church of which Paul said, "In everything ye are enriched by Him, in all utterance, and in all knowledge so that ye come behind in no gift" (1 Corinthians 1:5,7).

They abounded in everything, and yet sadly lacked love. This sad spectacle teaches us how the natural powers of the soul, knowledge, faith, and utterance may be mightily affected without self being entirely surrendered. Thus many of the gifts of the Spirit may be seen, while the chief of them all, love, is sadly lacking.

It is not enough for the Spirit to take hold of these natural gifts of the soul and exercise them in God's service. Something more is needed. The Spirit has entered the soul, so that through it He may obtain influence in both soul and spirit. Then, with self deposed, God may reign. The sign which indicates that self is deposed and that God does reign will be *love*—the surrender and the power to consider nothing as life except love, a life in the love of the Spirit.

Let us ask God to teach His people that a church or a Christian professing to have the Holy Spirit must first prove it by the exhibition of Christlike love. The life of Christ will be seen in its gentleness in bearing wrong and in its life of self-sacrifice to overcome the wrong. The life of Christ must be repeated in His members.

Receiving Love

The Spirit is indeed the love of God come down to us. We have that love within our reach. It is indeed dwelling within us. Since the day we were sealed with the Holy Spirit, the love of God has been shed abroad in our hearts. Though there may have been little to see of it in our lives, and though we hardly knew it, it was there. Along with the Holy Spirit came the love of God into our hearts. The two could never be separated.

If we want to experience this blessing, we must begin by a very simple faith in what the Word says. The Word is Spirit-breathed, the divinely-prepared organ through which the Spirit reveals what He is and does. As we take that Word as divine truth, the Spirit will make it truth in us.

Water descends in rain, flows out as streams, then rises up to heaven again as a vapor—still it is all one. So is the love of God in its threefold form—His love for us, our love for Him, and our love for each other as brethren. The love of God is within you by the Holy Spirit. Believe it and rejoice in it. Yield yourself to it as a divine fire consuming the sacrifice and lifting it heavenward. Exercise and practice this love in your relationships with everyone on earth. Then you will understand and prove that the Spirit of God is the love of God.

The way by which the Spirit works any virtue in believers is by stirring us to do it. The Spirit of God does not effectually work love, or give strength to love, until we act upon it. We cannot see or feel any such thing as love for God or man in our hearts before we act with love. We do not know our spiritual strength unless we use and exercise it. "The love of God is shed abroad in our hearts through the Holy Ghost which is given unto us" (Romans 5:5).

The love is there, but we may remain ignorant of it unless we believe that we have the power to love God and man with our whole heart. Faith and obedience always precede the conscious enjoyment and experience of the Spirit's power. Just as God is love to you, you must be love to everyone around you.

Keep the two sides of this truth in harmony. Wait in God's Holy Presence for the quickening of your faith that the Holy Spirit does dwell in you and fill you with love. On the other hand, give yourself, apart from what you feel, to a whole-hearted obedience to the command of love. Act out the gentleness and forbearance, the kindness and helpfulness, and the self-sacrifice and goodness of Christ Jesus.

Live in the love of Jesus, and you will be a messenger of His love to everyone you meet. The more intimate your communion with Jesus through the Holy Spirit, the more accurate will your translation of that life be into the relationships of daily life.

The compensation for our not being able to see God is this: *we have one another to love!* (See 1 John 3:14-24.) If we do this, God lives in us! We do not have to ask if our brother is worthy: God's love for us and for him is love for the unworthy. It is with this divine love that the Holy Spirit fills us and teaches us to love the brethren.

Prayer

Lord Jesus, look upon Your Church, look upon our hearts. And, wherever You see that there is not love like Yours, deliver us from all that is still selfish and unloving. Teach us to crucify self which cannot love. Teach us to believe that we can love, because the Holy Spirit has been given to us. Teach us to begin to love and serve, to sacrifice self and live for others.

May love with action be increased and perfected in us. Teach us to believe that because You live in us, Your love is in us, too. Now, we can love as You do, Lord Jesus. Amen.

Chapter 28

THE UNITY OF THE SPIRIT

"That ye walk. . .With all lowliness and meekness, with longsuffering, forbearing one another in love; Endeavouring to keep the unity of the Spirit in the bond of peace. There is one body, and one Spirit"—Ephesians 4:1-4.

"Now there are diversities of gifts, but the same Spirit. . . .But all these worketh that one and the self same Spirit, dividing to every man severally as he will. . . .For by one Spirit are we all baptized into one body. . .and have been all made to drink into one Spirit"—1 Corinthians 12:4,11,13.

In the first three chapters of Ephesians, Paul sets forth the glory of Christ Jesus as the Head of the Church and the glory of God's grace in the Church as the Body of Christ. The Body of Christ is indwelt by the Holy Spirit, growing up into a habitation of God through the Spirit. The Church is destined to be filled with all the fullness of God. Paul lifts the believer to his true place in the heavenlies, with his life hid in Christ.

In the second half of the epistle, Paul teaches how he is to walk worthy of his calling. The very first lesson he has to give in regard to this life and walk on earth (Ephesians 4:1-4) rests on the truth that the Holy Spirit has united him not only to Christ in heaven, but to Christ's Body on earth. The Spirit dwells in Christ in heaven, in the believer on earth, and most especially in Christ's Body, with all its members.

The full, healthy action of the Spirit can only be found where the right relationship exists between the individual and the whole Body. The believer's first concern in his Christian walk must be to see that the unity of the Spirit is maintained. If this unity of the one Spirit and one Body was fully acknowledged, the main virtue of the Christian life would be lowliness and meekness. (See Ephesians 4:2,3.)

Each person would forget and give up self for others. Everyone would be patient with one another in love amid all differences and shortcomings. In this way, the new commandment would be kept, and the Spirit of love would sacrifice itself completely for others.

The first epistle to the Corinthians remarkably illustrates the need for such teaching. In that church, there were abundant operations of the workings of the Holy Spirit. The gifts of the Spirit were strikingly manifested, but the fruit of the Spirit was remarkably absent.

They did not understand how there are diversities of gifts, but the same Spirit. They did not understand, amid all their differences, that one and the same Spirit bestows to each as He wills. They did not understand how all had been baptized in one Spirit into one Body and all made to drink of one Spirit. They did not know the more excellent way and that the chief of all the gifts of the Spirit is the love that does not seek its own way. Love finds its life and its happiness in others.

To each believer who longs for the power of the indwelling Spirit, the *unity of the Spirit* is a rich, spiritual blessing. In previous writings, I have used the expression of Pastor Stockmaier: "Have a deep reverence for the work of the Holy Spirit within you." That assertion needs as its complement a second one: have a deep reverence for the work of the Holy Spirit in your brother.

This is no easy thing. Even Christians, advanced in other respects, often fail here. The cause is not difficult to discover. In our books on education we are taught that discrimination, the observing of differences, is one of the earliest to be developed in children. The power of observing the harmony that exists amid apparent diversity is a higher skill and comes later.

This lesson can be seen in the Christian life and Church. A little grace is only needed to know where we differ from other Christians or churches. It is easy to point out our views or to judge their errors in doctrine or conduct. But grace always gives the unity of the Spirit the first place. Grace has faith in the power of love to maintain the living union amid outward separation.

Keeping The Unity Of The Spirit

Keep the unity of the Spirit. This is God's command to every believer. It is the new commandment—to love one another. If you would obey the command, note carefully that it is the *unity of the Spirit*. There is a unity of creed and denomination in which the bond is more of the flesh than of the Spirit. If you want to keep the unity of the Spirit, remember the following things.

Seek to know the unity of the Spirit in yourself. There is much in you that is of self, and the flesh, and that can take part in a unity that is of this earth. However, this will greatly hinder the unity of the Spirit. Confess that it is not in your own power or love that you can love. All that is of yourself is selfish and does not reach the true unity of the Spirit.

Be very humble in the thought that it is only what is of God in you that can ever unite with what appears displeasing to yourself. Be very joyful in the thought that the Spirit in you can conquer self, and you can love even what seems unlovable.

Study also to know the unity of the Spirit in your brother with whom you are to be united. There is in him a hidden seed of the divine life, surrounded by much that is carnal and often very trying and displeasing. This requires the humble knowledge of how unworthy you yourself are and the loving readiness to excuse your brother. Jesus did this on His last night: "the spirit indeed is willing, but the flesh is weak" (Matthew 26:41).

Look persistently at what there is in your brother of the image and Spirit of the Father. Do not value him by what he is in himself, but by what he is in Christ. Then you will feel how the same life and Spirit is in him, too. In this way the unity of the Spirit will triumph over the difference and dislike of the flesh. The Spirit in you, acknowledging and meeting the Spirit in your brother, will bind you in the unity of a life that is from above.

Keep this unity of the Spirit by having fellowship with other believers. The bond between the members of my body is most living and real, maintained by the circulation of the blood and the life it carries. "In one Spirit we were all baptized into one body." "There is one body and one Spirit." The inner union of life must find expression and be strengthened in the manifested communion of love.

Do not fellowship only with those who are of the same way of thinking and worshipping as yourself. Let your unity be more in the Spirit than in the flesh. In all your thoughts and judgments of other believers, practice the love that thinks no evil. Never say an unkind word of a child of God. Love every believer, not because he agrees with you or is pleasing to you, but because the Spirit of the Father is in him.

Give yourself to love and labor for God's children who, through ignorance, weakness, or waywardness, do not know that they have the Spirit within them. The work of the Spirit is to build up a habitation for God. Yield yourself to the Spirit in you to do the work. Recognize your dependence upon the fellowship of the Spirit in your brother and his dependence upon you. Seek your growth and his in the unity of love.

Unity In The Church

Take part in the united intercession that rises up to God for the unity of His Church. Continue the intercession of the Great High Priest for all believers to be one. The Church is *one* in the life of Christ and the love of the Spirit. Unfortunately, it is not *one* in the manifested unity of the Spirit. Thus the need for the command: keep the unity. Plead with God for the mighty working of His Spirit in all countries, churches, and believers.

When the tide is low, each little pool along the shore with its inhabitants is separated from the other by a rocky barrier. As the tide rises, the barriers are flooded over and all meet in one great ocean. So it will be with the Church of Christ. As the Spirit of God comes, according to the promise, as a flood upon the dry ground, each believer will disappear as the Spirit is known and honored.

How is this change to be brought about? Christ prayed that we all may be one. How is this to be fulfilled? Let each of us begin with himself. Resolve even now that this will be the one mark of your life. The proof of your sonship will be having and knowing the indwelling Spirit. If you are to unite with what the Spirit in you sees and seeks in others, you must yield yourself to His way of thinking and acting.

If you are to do this, the Spirit must have the mastery of your whole being. You need to abide in the living and never-ceasing consciousness that He dwells within you. You need to pray unceasingly that the Father may grant you, according to the riches of His glory, to be strengthened with might by His Spirit in the inner man.

The Spirit will take full possession of your entire being in the faith of the Triune God. The Father gives the Spirit in the name of the Son, and the Spirit dwells within you. Our faith brings us into direct contact and fellowship with the Father and the Son. The fuller His indwelling and the mightier His working, the more truly spiritual your being becomes. The more self sinks away, the more the Spirit of Christ will use you to build up and bind together believers into an habitation of God.

Christ's Spirit will be in you, the holy anointing, to set you apart to be a messenger of the Father's love. You will have humility, gentleness, kindness, and forbearance of love amid all the differences and difficulties in the Church. With warmhearted sympathy and self-sacrifice you will go out to find and help all who need help. The Spirit in you will prove that He belongs to all the members of the Body as much as to you. Through you His love will reach out to everyone around you to teach and to bless.

The health of every member and even every particle of my body depends upon the health of the surrounding portion. The healing power of the healthy part must expel what is unhealthy, or the disease will spread. I am more dependent upon my brother than I know. He is more dependent on me than I know. The Spirit I have is the same Spirit of Christ dwelling in my brother.

To keep the unity of the Spirit by living in loving fellowship with believers around me is life in the Spirit. It has taken time, prayer, and faith to know the Spirit of God within you. It will take time, prayer, faith, and much love to know the Spirit of God in your brother.

Prayer

Blessed Lord, may every believer know the Spirit that is in him and is in his brother. In all lowliness and love, help us to keep the unity of the Spirit with those with whom we come into contact. May all the leaders of Your Church be enlightened from above. May the unity of the Spirit be more to them than all human bonds of union in creed or church order. May all who have put on the Lord Jesus above all things also put on love, the bond of perfectness.

Lord Jesus, draw Your people in united prayer to the footstool of Your throne of glory. Fill us with Your Spirit, and we shall be one—one Spirit and one Body. Amen.